# *Helping Students Cope with Divorce*

## A Complete Group Education and Counseling Program for Grades 7-12

Anne J. Spencer, Ph.D.

Robert B. Shapiro, Ph. D.

**THE CENTER FOR APPLIED
RESEARCH IN EDUCATION**
West Nyack, New York 10995

10 9 8 7 6 5 4 3 2 1

Library of Congress Cataloging-in-Publication Data

Spencer, Anne J.
    Helping students cope with divorce : a complete group
education and counseling program for grades 7-12 / by
Anne J. Spencer and Robert B. Shapiro.
        p.    cm.
    Includes bibliographical references.
    ISBN 0-87628-387-3
    1. Children of divorced parents—Counseling of. 2.
Group  counseling for children.  I. Shapiro, Robert B., 1944-
    II. Title.
    HQ777.5S62    1993
    373.14'6—dc20                                    93-22369
                                                          CIP

ISBN 0-87628-387-3

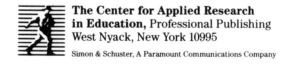

**The Center for Applied Research
in Education,** Professional Publishing
West Nyack, New York 10995

Simon & Schuster, A Paramount Communications Company

**Printed in the United States of America**

This book is dedicated to my parents
John and Jessie Spencer
for their patient support
through all the twists and turns of my life;

and to

Rachel Shapiro, Tracey Tepper, Ross Shapiro,
Cameron Shapiro, and Roni Tepper.

## ACKNOWLEDGMENTS

I would like to extend my thanks to Herbert Gordon for providing the inspiration for the research that led to the development of this program. I would also like to thank Gretchen Brayley for her assistance in establishing the program and Gregory Waas and Karen Stoiber for their technical assistance. A special thank you is in order to Kathy Rettig for her assistance in the typing of the manuscript. Most importantly, I wish to thank the many high school students who shared their divorce experiences with me and who participated in the research that supports the present program.

*Anne J. Spencer*

For a large portion of my professional life I have worked with divorcing families and, in particular, children of divorce. I have always been impressed with their candor, and at times, the power of their defensiveness. Their pain has tugged at my sensitivities and their incredible resilience has amazed me. More than any textbooks I have read or workshops I have attended, they have taught me to be a better parent and a better evaluator. They have sharpened my skills and increased my sensitivity while at the same time, affected my ideas about custody and visitation. I am greatly indebted to these hundreds of children for helping me grow as a professional. It is because of this that I dedicate this book to the children of divorce whom I know best—my own.

I also wish to thank my wife, Dayle Shapiro, whose continued support of my writing and her sacrifices for my career, are greatly appreciated. The thank you's are not said often enough, but the appreciation is deeply felt. My thanks also go to Sheila Jacobson, my secretary, whose dedication to me, my work, and the patients in the office make my life easier and the lives of others around her more comfortable.

*Robert B. Shapiro*

## ABOUT THE AUTHORS

***Anne J. Spencer*** is a school psychologist with Cooperative Association for Special Education, which provides psychological services for member districts in Central DuPage County schools in Illinois. She has worked with children ages 3 to 21 while practicing psychology as an associate in a private practice and is currently serving one high school and two elementary schools. She holds degrees from Northern Illinois University in DeKalb, Illinois, where she has also taught psychology courses.

***Robert B. Shapiro*** is a psychologist and director of a private practice, Dr. Robert B. Shapiro and Associates in the Chicago metropolitan area. He is a member of the National Advisory Board for the Professional Academy of Custody Evaluators, author of *Separate Houses: A Practical Guide for Divorced Parents* by Prentice Hall Press, and has appeared on national television, including talk shows such as The Oprah Winfrey Show. He earned his Ph.D. in psychology from DePaul University in Chicago and taught child development as an assistant professor in the Department of Psychiatry for the Medical School at the University of Illinois.

*About This Resource*

# Effects of Divorce on Education

History has taught us that educational institutions intervene when society does not adequately handle the problems of its children and adolescents; consequently, sex education, education about smoking and alcohol and drug abuse have all become the responsibility of our schools during the past two decades. Now these schools are newly challenged by the problems that children of divorce present to the academic community.

Currently, between 45 and 50 percent of all marriages end in divorce. This trend is likely to continue into the 1990s and beyond. The number of children in the educational system who are experiencing divorce and its consequences is, therefore, significant. In many large metropolitan area school districts and those in the surrounding suburbs, more than half of the children are in single parent families or in blended families. With numbers of this magnitude and our knowledge of the destructiveness of divorce, every school should have an effective means of identifying and helping children who are struggling with issues of divorce.

## ☐ HOW THIS RESOURCE CAN HELP

*Helping Students Cope With Divorce* provides a systematic ten session program of education, counseling, and peer support. It provides adolescents with information about divorce, encourages the development of more effective coping skills, and facilitates the rebuilding of self-esteem as they struggle with their parents' divorce. The resource is written for the professional guidance counselor, school social worker, school psychologist, or other mental health professional who works regularly with adolescent aged children (11–18 years). The program is structured for professionals working within the educational system, but you can easily adapt it for work with adolescents in noneducational systems such as neighborhood youth centers, churches, or private practice.

To date, many therapeutic models have been developed to help children from divorced families. Books have been written to help adults cope better and to help educate adults about what their children may be experiencing and how to help the child adjust to the divorce. Books have been written for children to help them understand divorce. Finally, there are some packaged counseling programs, primarily for elementary-aged children, that exist. There is, however, very little for the adolescent whose parents are in the midst of a divorce crisis or who finds him- or herself struggling with the ongoing conflict of a prior divorce.

*Helping Students Cope With Divorce* provides the counselor with effective group techniques that focus on meeting the needs of adolescents. To adapt the sessions and the preparatory material to your use, the resource is divided into five main sections:

▲ Effects of divorce on children

▲ Establishing the group

▲ Treatment program (A ten session guide)

▲ Conclusions (Session results)

▲ Counseling, education, and ancillary programs

Although the focus of the resource is the ten-session treatment program, you, as the group leader, or the person you select to be the leader, will want to study Sections 1 and 2 first to prepare you for leading the sessions.

**Section 1** includes background on the effects of divorce on children by reviewing literature, studies, and research on the problem. It covers problems common to children of divorce and supplies you with some helpful tools, in reproducible form, to determine the level of developmental adjustment and estimate the destructiveness of the divorce for individual students in the group. It also outlines treatment components and gives case studies in divorce experiences.

**Section 2** provides effective group techniques that focus on meeting the needs of adolescents. It supplies guidance for understanding the processes that occur in the initial, middle, and termination stages of group therapy and suggests therapy techniques that may be useful during these stages. It also helps you identify students in need of this therapy and offers practical suggestions for forming and managing the groups.

**Section 3** is the guide to the treatment program in ten sessions, which will be discussed in more detail in the pages that follow.

**Section 4** discusses the possibility and value of continuing the program beyond ten weeks. After reviewing background studies about the long-term effects of divorce, conclusions are drawn about the resulting behaviors in adult children of divorce.

**Section 5** a brief summary, promotes in-service training for teachers to heighten their sensitivity to problems of children of divorce and suggests ways to provide training without cost.

# ☐ THE TREATMENT PROGRAM

Each of the ten group sessions has a specific goal and guides the counselor, step by step, toward that goal. The resource does this by providing examples of what to say and how to get the students to participate, and by supplying suggested "minilectures" and examples of useful analogies and metaphors. Session by session, all these aids help the counselor develop trust with the group members and between the group members.

Another important part of this program is that it helps students understand how their environment affects their self-image, and how parent's moods and behaviors can affect children's self-evaluations. In conjunction, group participants learn how to cope more effectively with conflict and stress.

The session guide also shows you how to help students make sense out of the many volatile emotions created by divorce and teach them strategies for managing these emotions. You will help them enhance their coping skills and teach them problem-solving skills that they can apply to the real life situations created by their parents' divorce.

Selected group sessions focus on issues such as resolving interpersonal conflicts, coping with inner conflict, and dealing with problems unique to children from divorced families. Group participants also discuss issues that arise from parental dating, remarriage, and the blending of families. Students talk about their own ability to form meaningful relationships with parents, friends, and boyfriends/girlfriends. The entire program targets the enhancement of self-esteem.

# ☐ BEYOND THE BASIC PROGRAM

In addition to the basic program, this resource offers suggestions for establishing an ongoing support group for adolescents who have completed the initial ten sessions. The discussion focuses on the rationale for such continued support and includes topics such as how to combine groups upon program completion and how to introduce or withdraw single individuals from ongoing groups.

# ☐ LIMITATIONS OF THE PROGRAM

Divorce can have a devastating effect on the developmental process in children. The purpose of *Helping Students Cope With Divorce* is to help students develop strategies that will enable them to cope more effectively with conflict and frustration, and refocus on their academic, social, and personal pursuits. Collectively, the sessions provide a system through which the students can begin to rebuild their damaged self-concept and self-esteem. Although the program presented in this resource teaches skills that help facilitate a return to the normal developmental pattern, it does not cure deep-seated emotional problems. It should, therefore, not be viewed as a substitute for individual or family psychotherapy although it can be an effective adjunct to these processes.

We hope this treatment program will help your students as much as it has ours.

*Anne Spencer*

*Bob Shapiro*

# CONTENTS

**ABOUT THIS RESOURCE  9**

Effects of Divorce on Education  9
How This Resource Can Help  9
The Treatment Program  11
Beyond the Basic Program  11
Limitations of the Program  11

**SECTION 1:  EFFECTS OF DIVORCE ON CHILDREN  19**

ABOUT SELF-ESTEEM  19

Self-Esteem and the Family  20
Self-Esteem and Change  20
Self-Esteem and Groups  20

BACKGROUND: EFFECTS OF PARENTAL DIVORCE  21

Statistics on Divorce  21
Review of Research on the Effects of Parental Divorce  22

COMMON CONCERNS OF CHILDREN OF DIVORCE  23

Fear  23
Sadness or Loss  23
Feelings of Responsibility  25
Lonliness  25
Rejection  25
Conflicting Loyalties  26
Anger  26

OTHER FACTORS INFLUENCING EXPRESSION OF THE RESPONSE TO DIVORCE  26

Using the Adjustment Scale  26
*Adjustment Scale R1-1*  27
Divorce Destructiveness Scale  29
Behavioral Response to Divorce  29
*Divorce Destructiveness Scale R1-2*  30

TREATMENT COMPONENTS 33

Self-Esteem 33
Cognitive Component 35
Coping 36
Other Areas Affected 37

CASE STUDIES IN DIVORCE EXPERIENCES 37

Devastating Divorce 37
Case Study—Jim 37
Destructive Divorce 39
Case Study—Becky 39
Case Study—David 40
Benevolent Divorce 40
Case Study—Jenny 40
Importance of Belonging 41
Meeting Students' Needs With This Program 41

**SECTION 2: ESTABLISHING AND MANAGING THE GROUP 43**

BEGINNING A SUPPORT GROUP 43

Appropriate Settings for Groups 43
Appropriate Group Leaders 44
Checklist for Forming Groups 45
Identifying Students of Divorce 45
*Checklist for Forming Divorce Groups R2-1* 46
Which Students Should Be Invited to Participate? 47
Student Interview 48
Number and Age Range of Participants 48
*Student Identification Form R2-2* 49
*Letter to Parents R2-3* 51
Scheduling the Groups 52
*Teacher Notification Form R2-4* 53
Topical Approach to Sessions 54
Termination or Continuation? 54
Adding Students to an Established Group 55

GROUP THEORY 56

INITIAL STAGE 56

Participant Fears 56
Resistance 56
Content Versus Process 57
Respect and Genuineness 59
Speaking and Active Listening 59
Arranging the Room 59
Qualities of a Good Speaker 60
Qualities of a Good Listener 60

MIDDLE STAGE 61

    Empathizing and Clarifying 62
    Transference 62
    Confronting the Belief System 63
    Interpretive Statements 64
    Defenses 64
    Intense Sessions 64

TERMINATION STAGE 65

**SECTION 3: TREATMENT PROGRAM: A TEN-SESSION GUIDE 67**

SESSION ONE: INTRODUCTION AND RATIONALE FOR GROUP PARTICIPATION 69

    Goals 69
    Strategy 69
    Rationale 69
    Steps I–VIII 71
        *Who I Am Self-Esteem Scale R3-1* 74
        *Evaluation Form—Session One R3-2* 78

SESSION TWO: SELF-ESTEEM 81

    Goal 81
    Strategy 81
    Rationale 81
    Steps I–IV 83
        *Evaluation Form—Session Two R3-3* 87

SESSION THREE: TRUST, FEELINGS, AND SHARING SELF AND FEELINGS 91

    Goals 91
    Strategy 91
    Rationale 91
    Steps I, II 93
        *Evaluation Form—Session Three R3-4* 98

SESSION FOUR: PROBLEM SOLVING 101

    Goal 101
    Strategy 101
    Rationale 101
    Steps I–IV 102
        *Six Steps for Problem Solving R3-5* 104
        *Evaluation Form—Session Four R3-6* 105

SESSION FIVE: PERSONAL RIGHTS 109

    Goals 109
    Strategy 109
    Rationale 109

Steps I–V  111
   *Your Rights as an Individual R3-7*  113
   *Personal Rights for Children of Divorce R3-8*  114
   *What You Can Do When Your Rights Have Been Violated R3-9*  115
   *Evaluation Form—Session Five R3-10*  117

SESSION SIX: WORKING THROUGH CONFLICT  121

Goals  121
Strategy  121
Rationale  121
Steps I–IV  122
   *Working Through Conflict R3-11*  123
   *Evaluation Form—Session Six R3-12*  124

SESSION SEVEN: INNER CONFLICT AND RELAXATION TRAINING  127

Goal  127
Strategy  127
Rationale  127
Steps I–IV  128
   *Relaxation Instructions R3-13*  130
   *Sample Dialogue for an Extended Relaxation Training Session R3-14*  131
   *Evaluation Form—Session Seven R3-15*  133

SESSION EIGHT: PROBLEMS UNIQUE TO CHILDREN OF DIVORCED FAMILIES  137

Goal  137
Strategy  137
Rationale  137
Steps I–IV  138
   *Evaluation Form—Session Eight R3-16*  140

SESSION NINE: DATING, REMARRIAGE, AND THE STEPFAMILY  143

Goal  143
Strategy  143
Rationale  143
Steps I–IV  145
   *Evaluation Form—Session Nine R3-17*  147

SESSION TEN: HOPES FOR THE FUTURE, RELATIONSHIP BUILDING, GROUP TERMINATION  151

Goals  151
Strategy  151
Rationale  151
Steps I–VI  152
   *Leader Evaluation Form—Session Ten R3-18*  155

FUTURE SESSIONS  159

Goal  159
Strategy  159
*Evaluation Form—Treatment Program R3-19*  161
*Student Evaluation Form R3-20*  164

**SECTION 4:  CONCLUSIONS  165**

Session Results  165
Continuing the Program  165

Background: Long-Term Effects of Divorce  166
Contributing Factors to Long-Term Effects  167
The Overburdened Child  167
Children Responsible for Their Own Care  167
Children Responsible for a Parent  168
Children in the Shadow of Their Parents' Conflicts  168

Drawing Conclusions from Research  169
Case Study—Dana  169

Resulting Behaviors in Adult Children of Divorce  170
Anger  170
Relationship Problems  171
Feelings of Separation  171
Feelings of Dependency  172
Sense of Esteem  172
Devaluing of the Family System  172
Loss of Sense of Belonging  173
The Myth of Divorce  173

**SECTION 5:  COUNSELING, EDUCATION, AND ANCILLARY PROGRAMS  175**

School Focus on Whole Development of Child  175

In-Service Training for Teachers  176

Feedback Welcome  176

**REFERENCES  177**

**BIBLIOGRAPHY AND SUGGESTED READING  179**

**FORMS  183**

*Section 1*

# Effects of Divorce on Children

The effects of divorce on children can be devastating. As parents pull away from each other they become increasingly preoccupied with their own survival. Although their thoughts and plans may include the children (especially for the custodial parent), the process of planning is generally solitary or takes place in conversation with other adults. Most children have little understanding of why their parents are getting divorced. A child's sense of security and well-being can be terribly threatened by the prospect of a divorce. The knowledge that they will be able to see only one parent at a time and the loss of a sense of family are very frightening. The process of both parents becoming more self-absorbed as the divorce develops brings a painful sense of reality to their fears.

Living in a heightened state of anxiety and fear can seriously damage children's self-esteem. Their ability to stay on task, concentrate, and persevere diminishes. They are frustrated easily. They become more vulnerable to the pain of disappointment, broken promises, failure at school, and the many fluctuations in peer relationships. All these conditions erode their self-esteem and increase their fear and anxiety. The people they depend on the most to help them cope and feel better about themselves are not available. This negative spiral and the incumbent damage to the child's self-esteem system can last from a number of months to many years. In fact, some children never fully recover from the devastating effects of their parents' divorce.

## ABOUT SELF-ESTEEM

Damage to the child's self-esteem may be the single most devastating effect of parental divorce. In its beginning, self-esteem starts off as well-being; a physical and psychological sense of well-being. This is nurtured primarily by the mother-child relationship. Through her care and attention, the child feels satisfied.

Momentary discomforts such as hunger, cold, and wet are removed by her caring. The sense of well-being that she provides in these early months is the essence or core of the self-esteem system. The child feels valued; this powerful person, mother, feels that the child is important enough to be cared for.

### Self-Esteem and the Family

As the child develops, other people, the child's family, also provide esteem enhancing experiences. Father and mother, and perhaps siblings, applaud the child's successes, encourage his/her efforts, and provide comfort when the child experiences pain. A child's first remembered experiences regarding his or her self-worth come from the immediate family. The family is the "source group" for the child's self-esteem.

> Man wishes to be confirmed in his being by man, and wishes to have a presence in the being of the other. The human person needs confirmation, because man as man needs it. An animal does not need to be confirmed, for it is what it is, unquestionably. It is different with man: sent forth from the natural domain of species into the hazard of the solitary category, surrounded by the dirge and chaos which came into being with him, secretly and bashfully he watches for a YES which allows him to be and which can come to him only from one human person to another. It is from one man to another that the heavenly bread of self-being is passed. —— **Martin Buber**

### Self-Esteem and Change

As the years go by and development continues, many changes occur that affect the valuing process and hence the child's self-esteem. Grandparents (or other family members) may die, a favorite aunt or babysitter may move away, or new children may be born. These numerous changes together with the child's own abilities and emerging personality influence the kind of responses and experiences that the self-esteem building group will provide for the child. However, the basic element that formed this group, the mother and father (family), still remains. Consequently, despite the occasional loss that traumatizes the child (such as a death or the loss of a loved one), the child survives and continues to develop.

As this development continues, self-esteem becomes less dependent on outside reinforcement and more responsive to rational self-appraisal. This process continues until adulthood, when self-esteem is based for the most part on our ability to be consistent with our self-concept and less on the appraisal of others.

### Self-Esteem and Groups

As the child develops through preadolescence (ages 11 and 12 years) and adolescence (ages 13-18), tremendous strides are made physically and intellectually. With these strides the child moves in and out of many new groups, usually staying with those groups that provide the most rewards and reinforcement (the adolescent counterpart of the infant's sense of well-being). Some of the more common groups are sports teams, scout groups, music groups, church groups, various community clubs and organizations, and a general peer group that may be made up of kids from one or many of the groups just mentioned. Children have varying experiences within these groups. Some of these experiences are positive, some are negative. Throughout preadolescence and adolescence, children may move in and out of as many as five or six major groups. Adolescence is a critical time. The child's self-esteem, established primarily within the family, is now tested as the child begins the task of separating from the family. Rapid physical changes, intellectual growth, interest in the opposite sex, all force the adolescent to assess and reassess "Who am I?" and "How capable am I?"

The adolescents who have had positive self-esteem building experiences within the family will handle these adolescent experiences much better. Throughout all of the changes that occur as the adolescent moves from one group to another, one stabilizing factor, the family, remains constant. The family is, generally, available to move back to as the primary source of affirmation and acknowledgment, and of support and validation. When things get scary, when sexual pressures, or pressures to drink, or pressures to change appearance get too intense, the support of the family is always there. In normal adolescent development, children alternately take strides toward self-determination and becoming dependent again.

However, if the preadolescent or adolescent is experiencing parental divorce or even if the parents were divorced years earlier, the support and affirmation of the family may not be there. The normal anxiety-provoking experiences of adolescence can now take on terrifying proportions. Robbed of the self-esteem building acknowledgment from the family, the adolescent may become vulnerable to the negative influence of certain groups (drinking, drugs, sexual promiscuity). With the dissolution of the family there develops a tendency to question, even doubt, the values espoused by the family. After all, if the family was so good, if the values were so right, why didn't it remain? With the underpinning source of affirmation and acknowledgment destroyed, doubts about self and values can develop. If not defined by the sense of family, who is the child? Nobody?

The increased vulnerability of the self-esteem system that occurs when parents divorce can result in poor academic performance and poor social adjustment during the stage of adolescent development. As we have suggested, the group treatment program in this resource will provide students with a new source group for building self-esteem.

## ☐ BACKGROUND: EFFECTS OF PARENTAL DIVORCE

### Statistics on Divorce

The incidence of divorce in American society has steadily increased since World War II, leveling off during the last decade at about 48 percent (for every 100 marriages that take place, 48 married couples are getting divorced). It appears now that this 48 percent divorce rate will continue throughout the 1990s. According to the United States Bureau of the Census (1990), there were 1,163,000 divorces in 1989 involving 1,038,000 children. The national divorce rate more than doubled between 1970 and 1981 and has more than tripled since 1960 giving the United States the dubious distinction of having the highest divorce rate in the world. Approximately 11 million, or one out of five children, are currently living in single parent homes. The magnitude of the problem is astounding.

What, in part, has fueled this sharp rise in divorce was the misconception that although divorce is traumatic for children, they will survive. Consequently, adults have felt increasingly more comfortable pursuing their own needs. The past 30 years have produced hundreds of thousands of children of divorce and their experiences are teaching us a great deal about the impact divorce has on our young people. Divorce is clearly traumatic for children and we are discovering that if it is not handled properly, it has the potential for permanently scarring their lives. For example, two-thirds of all adolescent admissions to psychiatric hospitals are children of divorce.

## Review of Research on the Effects of Parental Divorce

Many psychologists initially described divorce as a brief crisis producing effects that disappeared with the passage of time. This idea was based in part on certain symptoms that often accompanied the child's initial response to the divorce crisis. For example, younger children may develop school related problems such as difficulty in concentrating. Because symptoms commonly disappear within a few years, it was believed that the effects of divorce dissipated with the symptoms. Several recent longitudinal studies, however, indicate that the psychological effects of divorce are more far reaching than was expected previously. For example, at the 5-year mark of her study, Wallerstein (1980) reported that although one-third of the children in her study appeared to be doing well, another third were clearly deteriorating, exhibiting such symptoms as acting out behaviors, sleep disturbances, and poor school performance.

Many researchers now agree that the effects of divorce can be better understood if divorce is viewed as a chain of events rather than as a single crisis. This chain may begin with marital conflict prior to the divorce, and be followed by disorganization associated with the actual separation and divorce, changes in the family structure (loss of a parent), one or more relocations, changes in parental relationships (the child may be encouraged to be supportive of one parent while rejecting the other), changes in or loss of peer relationships, and the possible introduction of new relationships (stepparents, stepsiblings). Some researchers suggest that it is not the actual parent/child separation that is detrimental to the child's psychological well-being, but rather the prior and continuing family disharmony. Each of these events represents a complex set of variables that, along with the child's own coping skills and support systems, can determine the psychological effect that the divorce will have on the child.

Much of the research on the effects of divorce and on the treatment for children of divorce has focused on elementary-aged children. Yet adolescents may be one of the most needy age groups because the divorce experience interacts with the complex developmental tasks that all teenagers must cope with. For example, parental divorce during adolescence may interfere with the normal developmental process. Adolescent-aged children must deal with issues of developing an individual identity, developing emotional attachments outside of the family, and separation from the family. They use the family as a secure base, alternating between having close contact and pulling away. When divorce disrupts this base, the adolescent may be thrust into a state of "psuedomaturity" (Sorosky, 1977) which may be expressed through sexual acting out behaviors or power struggles with adult authority figures. For children who experience divorce during their elementary school years, conflicts stemming from the divorce may first begin to emerge during adolescence. In addition to the developmental disruption, there is a higher incidence of alcohol and drug abuse and of delinquency among individuals from divorced families than from intact families making adolescents an especially at-risk population.

## ☐ COMMON CONCERNS OF CHILDREN OF DIVORCE

Although the child's developmental level interacts with situational variables to determine the specific response to the divorce, Wallerstein and Kelly (1980) outlined themes or concerns that appear to be common to most children of divorce, regardless of age.

### Fear

First, divorce is a frightening experience. Although the fear may be real or imagined and the specific content is variable, the underlying concern is one of vulnerability and abandonment. Many children of divorce appear to believe that if the marriage can dissolve, so too can the parent/child relationship. Children may express concern over who will care for them, feed them, and provide such "tangibles" as clothes and college educations.

A sense of the unknown further compounds the child's fear. Wallerstein found that, although one-third of the children in her study had experienced threats of divorce prior to the actual event, another one-third had little awareness of parental unhappiness prior to the decision to divorce. The announcement of the intent to divorce was most often brief and seldom accompanied by any explanation as to how the child would be affected. That is, children were not offered simple educational information about the meaning of divorce, nor were they encouraged to ask questions that may have helped clarify the concept of divorce in their own minds. Concerns about living arrangements, continuation of contact with both parents, and assurances of continued care and support were often not discussed. In most instances, Wallerstein reported that children were not encouraged to express their feelings about the situation.

### Sadness or Loss

A second concern, common among most children, is a sense of sadness or loss. For example, Wallerstein reported that many children in her study were openly

# CONCERNS COMMONLY IDENTIFIED
# IN CHILDREN'S RESPONSES TO DIVORCE

1. Fear

2. Sense of sadness and loss

3. Feelings of responsibility

4. Loneliness

5. Feelings of rejection

6. Conflicting loyalties

7. Anger

**Figure 1-1.** Wallerstein and Kelly, as well as other researchers, have identified certain themes which are common concerns among children who are experiencing parental divorce.

tearful or moody. Frequently the children showed acute depressive symptoms such as sleep disturbances and difficulty in sustaining attention. Younger children (preschool and early elementary-aged) were most concerned with the departure of the father, while older children and adolescents focused on the breakdown of the family and the continuity and structure that the family had provided. Most children wished to maintain contact with the absent parent and hoped for reconciliation between their parents.

### Feelings of Responsibility

A third concern is that children of divorce may become burdened by feeling responsible for the well-being of one or both parents. Parents, coping with the radical changes taking place in their lives, frequently become entangled in their own emotional distress. Their attention is focused on their own troubles and anxieties. As a result of this increased stress, parents may be inconsistent and less affectionate toward their children. Divorcing parents commonly experience depression, making it difficult to offer comfort to the child. It is not uncommon for both parents to treat older children, particularly adolescent-aged children, as confidants. The parent may express their own fears, sharing not only economic and logistical concerns, but also their own emotional distress, including suicidal thoughts. Often children respond to this form of parental distress by trying to become the caretaker of the parent, offering support and in some cases, attempting to effect a reconciliation. This is perhaps more poignant for an older, or adolescent child.

### Loneliness

The fourth concern centers on the loneliness that children of divorce often experience. As discussed previously, divorced parents are preoccupied and often inattentive to the emotional needs of their children. Typically, one parent (most often the father) leaves the household and the custodial parent must either begin working or work longer hours to compensate for lost income. Children are often left alone or with caretakers until the custodial parent returns from work. Those children and adolescents who have a prior history of poor adjustment and low self-esteem are likely to suffer the most in these instances. Well-functioning adolescents with good peer relations are the least likely to be lonely.

### Rejection

Feeling rejected is a fifth concern common to many children who experience parental divorce. The sense of rejection stems not only from the departure of the noncustodial parent, but also from the apparent withdrawal of interest in the child by the custodial parent. This sense of rejection may lead the child to question his/her own lovability and sense of self-worth. Wallerstein reported that as a group, 6- to 12-year-old boys in her study were the most likely to express feeling rejected by the departed father.

### Conflicting Loyalties

Children in divorcing families may be faced with the sixth concern of conflicting loyalties. Most children, regardless of age, wish to retain a relationship with both parents, yet many parents openly compete for their child's support and affection. One parent may try to form an alliance with the child against the other parent. If the child offers support to one parent, it pushes the child away from the other parent, increasing the sense of loneliness and rejection and making the child feel like a traitor.

### Anger

Anger is a seventh concern that characterizes many children of divorce. Almost all children are at risk for experiencing anger in one form or another. Wallerstein reported, for example, that the younger children (preschool and early elementary-aged) in her study were most likely to express the anger in such acting out behaviors as hitting or temper tantrums, often directed at other children. The older children (late elementary and adolescent-aged) were most likely to express the anger directly, through verbal attacks.

The degree and manner of expression for each of these themes varies from individual to individual. One factor found to influence this expression is the gender of the individual. For example, one research team found that boys from divorced families had greater behavioral, social, and academic difficulties than did boys from intact families (Guidubaldi, Cleminshaw, Perry, & Mcloughlin, 1983). Girls from divorced families were found to have fewer difficulties than boys from divorced families. This may be, in part, because most girls of divorce live with a highly influential female role model — their mother. Boys, however, typically do not live with the usual male role model — the father.

## ☐ OTHER FACTORS INFLUENCING EXPRESSION OF THE RESPONSE TO DIVORCE

The expression of these themes is also influenced by the child's prior level of adjustment (whether the level of functioning was appropriate for the child's developmental stage, prior to the divorce) and the destructiveness of the divorce itself.

### Using the Adjustment Scale

Adjustment varies along a continuum ranging from good to poor adjustment. Poorly adjusted individuals are more likely to exhibit a more negative response to parental divorce. The level of developmental adjustment can be estimated by completing the Adjustment Scale provided. Rate the student along each of the items on the scale. Most of the requested information can be obtained from school records or determined during an initial student interview. Assign a value of *one* to items in the left hand column, *two* to the items in the center column, and *three*

# ADJUSTMENT SCALE  R1-1

## (Instructor's sheet)

Please check the appropriate column. Rate the student's level of functioning *prior* to divorce.

1. What kind of student was the individual prior to the divorce (Was he/she attentive in class, did he/she complete assignments)?

   | _____ | _____ | _____ |
   |--------|--------|--------|
   | *poor* | *average* | *good* |

2. How was the student's attendance?

   | _____ | _____ | _____ |
   |--------|--------|--------|
   | *poor* | *average* | *good* |

3. What kind of grades did the student earn?

   | _____ | _____ | _____ |
   |--------|--------|--------|
   | *poor* | *average* | *good* |

4. Did the student attend  school functions or athletic events?

   | _____ | _____ | _____ |
   |--------|--------|--------|
   | *never* | *seldom* | *often* |

5. Did the student have any learning disabilities (such as a reading disability)?

   | _____ | _____ | _____ |
   |--------|--------|--------|
   | *severe* | *mild* | *none* |

6. Did the student have Attention Deficit-Hyperactivity Disorder?

   | _____ | _____ | _____ |
   |--------|--------|--------|
   | *severe* | *slight* | *none* |

7. Was the student socially accepted by the student population in general?

   | _____ | _____ | _____ |
   |--------|--------|--------|
   | *no* | *somewhat* | *yes* |

8. Did the student have close friendships?

   | _____ | _____ | _____ |
   |--------|--------|--------|
   | *no* | *average amount* | *yes* |

9. Was the student liked/accepted by the faculty?

   | _____ | _____ | _____ |
   |--------|--------|--------|
   | *no* | *somewhat* | *yes* |

10. Did the student spend a great deal of time alone?

    | _____ | _____ | _____ |
    |--------|--------|--------|
    | *yes* | *somewhat* | *no* |

11. Did the student have any physical handicaps?

    | _____ | _____ | _____ |
    |--------|--------|--------|
    | *yes* | *common ones such as glasses or braces* | *no* |

# ADJUSTMENT SCALE R1-1 (cont'd)
## (Instructor's sheet)

12. How was the student's health?

_____ _____ _____
*poor* *average* *good*

13. Rate the student's verbal skills.

_____ _____ _____
*poor* *average* *good*

14. Was the student involved in drug or alcohol abuse?

_____ _____ _____
*yes* *unknown* *no*

15. Was the student's dress similar to that of his/her peers?

_____ _____ _____
*bizarre* *average* *fashionable*

16. Did the student engage in unusual or bizarre behavior?

_____ _____ _____
*bizarre* *immature* *normal*

17. Rate the student's belief system.

_____ _____ _____
*bizarre* *immature* *well-structured*

18. Rate the student's organizational skills.

_____ _____ _____
*poor* *average* *good*

19. Did the student have plans for the future?

_____ _____ _____
*no* *vague* *well-defined*

20. Was the student aware of, and interested in, current events?

_____ _____ _____
*no* *somewhat* *yes*

to the items in the right hand column. Add the checked spaces to obtain the total adjustment score. The higher the score, the better the prior adjustment.

The destructive impact also varies along a continuum ranging from benevolent at the low end to devastating at the high end. The destructiveness of divorce can best be understood by examining the amount of change a student is forced to experience by his or her divorcing parents. The greater the amount of change, the more destructive the divorce experience for the student. We conceptualize change as occurring along the following two dimensions:

1. How much environmental change?

   ▲ Is there a change of residence?
   ▲ Is there a change of schools?
   ▲ Is there a change of community, town, or state?

2. How much familial change?

   ▲ Does the student have access to both parents?
   ▲ Did/do the parents blame each other in front of the student?
   ▲ Do the parents attend the student's activities?
   ▲ Was/is the student separated from a sibling?

### Divorce Destructiveness Scale

The group leader can estimate the destructiveness of divorce along these two dimensions by asking the student to complete the Divorce Destructiveness Scale that we have developed. The greater the number of negative responses, the greater the destructive impact of the divorce. The level of adjustment and the level of destructive impact combine to produce varying degrees of divorce impact.

Any divorce, even a benevolent divorce, will exacerbate the problems that a student is already experiencing. For example, a student who is struggling academically will experience even more difficulty scholastically in the aftermath of divorce. By the same token, a student who is having peer relationship difficulties prior to his or her parents' divorce will experience even more problems following divorce. However, no matter how benevolent a divorce is, a student with poor developmental adjustment will not cope as well as a student with good developmental adjustment. The feelings and emotions of fear, sadness and loss, feelings of responsibility, loneliness, feelings of rejection, conflicting loyalties, and anger increase dependent upon the child's prior developmental adjustment and the severity of the divorce situation. The intensity of these seven common responses is contingent upon the child's predivorce adjustment levels and the degree of divorce "devastation." *See Figure 1-2.*

### Behavioral Response to Divorce

Understanding the destructiveness of divorce and the child's developmental adjustment in conjunction with the seven most common concerns of children of

Name _____  Date _____

# DIVORCE DESTRUCTIVENESS SCALE R1-2

Please put an "X" in the appropriate column.

|  | Yes | No |
|---|---|---|
| 1. When your parents decided to get a divorce, did they separate between two weeks to two months after telling you about it? | _____ | _____ |
| 2. Did your parents tell you about the divorce together? | _____ | _____ |
| 3. Did your parents avoid blaming each other for the divorce? | _____ | _____ |
| 4. Do your parents avoid blaming each other now? | _____ | _____ |
| 5. Did your parents avoid fighting over custody? | _____ | _____ |
| 6. Were you asked to make a choice about which parent you wanted to live with? | _____ | _____ |
| 7. Did you remain in the same school after the divorce? | _____ | _____ |
| 8. Did you stay in your own home after the divorce? | _____ | _____ |
| 9. Immediately after the divorce, did the noncustodial parent (the one you do *not* live with) live within a half-hour's drive from your house? | _____ | _____ |
| 10. Does the noncustodial parent now reside within a half-hour's drive from your house? | _____ | _____ |
| 11. After the divorce, did you see the noncustodial parent at least 5 days out of the month? | _____ | _____ |
| 12. Do you now see the noncustodial parent on at least 5 days out of the month? | _____ | _____ |

# DIVORCE DESTRUCTIVENESS SCALE R1-2 (cont'd)

|  | Yes | No |
|---|---|---|
| 13. Do you talk to the noncustodial parent on the phone between visits? | _____ | _____ |
| 14. Is the parent who you live with supportive of visitation with the noncustodial parent? | _____ | _____ |
| 15. When you are with one parent, does he/she avoid making unpleasant comments about the other parent? | _____ | _____ |
| 16. Is the visitation schedule flexible? | _____ | _____ |
| 17. Do your parents avoid discussing money (such as child support) in front of you or with you? | _____ | _____ |
| 18. Does the parent with whom you live respond in a pleasant manner when you receive a gift from the noncustodial parent? | _____ | _____ |
| 19. Does the parent you live with attend activities that you participate in (such as athletic events or school plays)? | _____ | _____ |
| 20. Does the noncustodial parent attend such activities? | _____ | _____ |
| 21. Do you feel that your parents get along okay since the divorce? | _____ | _____ |
| 22. If you have brothers and/or sisters, do you all live together (or do some live with one parent and some with the other)? | _____ | _____ |
| 23. If you live with a stepparent, do you get along with the stepparent? | _____ | _____ |
| 24. If you live in a stepparent family, do you get along with stepbrothers and/or stepsisters? | _____ | _____ |
| 25. Have you received any type of counseling to help you with your parents' divorce? | _____ | _____ |

# FACTORS LIKELY TO INCREASE THE INTENSITY OF CONCERNS COMMON TO MOST CHILDREN OF DIVORCE

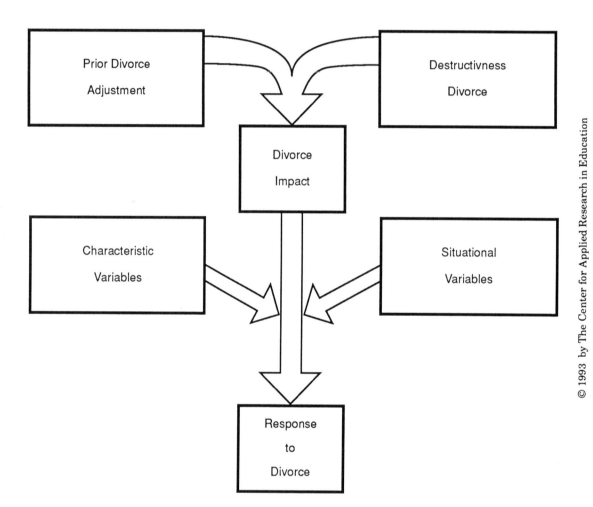

**Figure 1-2.** The child's prior level of adjustment and the destructiveness of the divorce combine to produce the divorce impact. The divorce impact, together with the child's characteristics (such as age, sex, and attitudes) and other situational variables determines the child's behavioral response to the divorce.

divorce will help you realize what a student is experiencing and what some of their needs might be. Figure 1-3 presents some of the common behavioral responses to divorce. All of these problems do not occur for every child of divorce. Any one student, however, may experience two, three, four, or more of them at a time. For example, a student who is experiencing depression following the parents' divorce may also become withdrawn and isolated, show an increase in absenteeism and demonstrate a sharp decline in academic performance. Another student, looking for support, may change peer groups, start drinking or increase his/her alcohol use, and become sexually active at even the junior high school level.

## ☐ TREATMENT COMPONENTS

Many researchers have stressed three aspects of adolescent functioning as essential targets of treatment programs:

▲ Self-esteem

▲ Cognitive understanding of divorce

▲ Coping skills

### Self-Esteem

All stages of child-adolescent development require the completion of certain tasks that move the student toward both separation and individuation, to adulthood. To complete these tasks, the student must maintain a level of self-esteem high enough to meet the challenges. That is, the student must have a positive estimate of his/her own self-worth. Divorce and its processes directly affect self-esteem in serious ways. Reduced parental support, doubt, insecurity, sense of distorted reality, inability to concentrate, increased vulnerability, and fear accompany almost all divorce situations. These factors reduce self-esteem in various ways.

---

**.Divorce creates emotional responses in children that may lower their self-esteem. This interferes with their ability to successfully meet developmental challenges and, consequently, may negatively affect their future self-concept.**

---

Self-esteem is developed early in life due to the love and support of significant others in the child's life and through the experience of competency in mastering life skills. It follows then, that children with high self-esteem come from families

# COMMON PROBLEMS AND BEHAVIORS
# FOR CHILDREN OF DIVORCE

1. Withdrawal and isolation

2. Depression

3. Increase in tardiness, absenteeism, and truancy

4. Sharp decline in academic performance

5. Dropping out of high school

6. Change in peer groups

7. Significant use of alcohol

8. Use of drugs

9. Early sexual experimentation

10. Sexual promiscuity

11. Pregnancy

12. Runaway

13. Fighting

14. Theft, vandalism, and other illegal behaviors

15. Suicide attempts

© 1993 by The Center for Applied Research in Education

**Figure 1-3**  Adolescents may manifest any of these or other behaviors as a response to parental divorce.

that provide a warm, accepting atmosphere for their children, that define and maintain clear limits within which their children must function, and that permit freedom for the children within the established limits. When family conflict reduces the child's perception of positive regard, security, and sense of control over his environment, the child's sense of self-worth will also be reduced.

We believe that self-esteem is hierarchical in nature. That is, the child monitors and evaluates his/her performance in many areas to form a more global opinion of his/her self-worth. Harter (1982) suggested that these evaluative judgments define the child's perception of competence in various areas. For example, social competence represents the child's perception of his/her success with peers. The child makes a higher order evaluation of his or her global self-worth based on perceived competency in areas that the child rates as important. For example, a child may perceive competence in peer relations as desirable. If peer relations are disrupted, as is often the case in divorced families, the child's perceived competence in this area may decline and reduce the child's global sense of self-worth.

The normal adolescent is focused on various developmental tasks such as the resolution of internal conflicts (control and expression of aggressive and sexual impulses), external conflicts (peer and social acceptance), and a need to gain independence from the family and establish an individual identity. Failure to resolve any of these conflicts (engaging in acting out behaviors, poor peer relations or failure to separate from the family conflict) may be perceived by the child as incompetence, which would then result in lowered self-esteem. For example, disruption of the adolescent's parental support system may lead to difficulties in resolving the normal adolescent issues of separation from the family.

Certain aspects of close-friend relationships such as intimacy and mutual acceptance are important in the development of adolescent self-esteem. Divorce may disrupt peer relationships. Disrupted relationships that impact at a time when these relationships are becoming increasingly important may inhibit normal social development and reduce self-esteem through failure to develop extrafamilial relationships and peer acceptance.

Divorce, then, affects self-esteem in the following ways:

▲ Reduced parental attention and positive regard
▲ Disruption of peer relationships and the associated peer support
▲ Perception of failure at developmental tasks.

Several studies have indeed found that adolescents from divorced families score lower on measures of self-esteem than those from intact families. The resultant lowered self-esteem makes it less likely that the individual will successfully master later developmental tasks.

## Cognitive Component

Knowledge of divorce provides children with a cognitive structure for thinking about divorce-related events and feelings. Some researchers have suggested the provision of common divorce information, such as statisical information and explanations of legal terms and normal divorce proceedings, helps to dispel misconceptions about divorce. Such information also helps children understand that divorce is a relatively common experience and that the problems and feelings they experience are frequently shared by others. Conversely, lacking knowledge of divorce or having erroneous information could lead the individual to misinterpret divorce-related events and hamper divorce-related problem-solving.

Wallerstein discussed divorce-related fears that stem from a sense of the unknown. Providing information about the meaning of divorce, about common divorce proceedings, and about often-experienced postdivorce events reduces the fear that is often created by a lack of knowledge about an event. In addition, the fear reduction serves to increase the child's sense of mastery over his/her environment.

### Coping

Coping refers to the behaviors that an adolescent uses to manage problems or relieve the discomfort associated with life changes. Having a variety of coping strategies in one's repertoire is important both for dealing directly with a problem and for dealing with the associated emotional stress. Thus, coping can be carried out cognitively or behaviorally. Generally children from divorced households have fewer adaptive coping skills available to them. As an example, a frequent coping reaction of adolescents dealing with divorce is early engagement in adult or "pseudoadult" activities. This may result in aggressive acting out behaviors or sexual promiscuity. Older adolescents may inappropriately engage in distancing and withdrawal from the family to avoid ongoing family conflict. The child must learn to develop coping strategies that will enable him/her to deal with the conflict, to solve problems, and to resume the normal course of development.

## Communication Skills

One effective means for increasing a child's coping capacity is to improve communication skills. This would include learning to recognize their rights as individuals and having them communicate to others when they believe their rights have been violated.

## Problem-Solving

A second means for enhancing coping capacity is through the teaching of problem-solving skills. Often, individuals from divorced families perceive the events of their lives as being beyond their control. Instruction in problem-solving should increase the individual's awareness of his/her own capacity to deal with problem situations and develop more effective problem-solving strategies.

## Stress Management

Many issues common to children who have experienced divorce appear to be emotionally based (fear, sense of loss, feelings of responsibility for the parent, loneliness, and anger). The child needs to develop skills to deal effectively with emotional stress. One such stress management technique is relaxation training. Relaxation training inhibits anxiety elicited during times of stress. This allows the individual to become a more effective problem solver and helps to reduce physiological arousal.

### Other Areas Affected

Not only can divorce affect the student's self-esteem and coping capacity, it can also affect the student's energy level, ability to persevere, stay on task, stay focused, concentrate, and memorize. These abilities are necessary for adequate academic performance and growth. Because divorce affects these abilities, academic performance is one of the most sensitive indicators of the divorce impact.

Academic performance may suffer in response to the degree of impact of the parental divorce. The greater the impact of divorce, the more likely it is that there will be a dramatic downturn in the student's school performance. Refer to *Figure 1-4.*

## ☐ CASE STUDIES IN DIVORCE EXPERIENCES

### Devastating Divorce

If a student with good developmental adjustment is fortunate, he/she will experience a less negatively affecting divorce situation (a benevolent divorce). The worst possibility would be the poorly adjusted student who is faced with a devastating divorce—one that produces significant environmental change combined with significant familial change. The essence of the devastating divorce is that the student feels separated and abandoned within his/her family while at the same time experiences significant estrangement from his/her sense of community.

### Case Study—Jim

Jim was a 14-year-old boy, the oldest of three children, of a couple who lived in a middle class suburb near Chicago. His parents' marital difficulties had been developing for the last three years. Finally, Dad left and the divorce began. The divorce necessitated the sale of the modest family home. As a result, Mom moved three suburbs away to a community in which one of her sisters lived. Jim, consequently, was in an unfamiliar community and started high school not knowing any of the students who attended that school. He left his entire peer group behind.

His mother, who had previously worked only part time, now worked a full-time job. Jim was therefore required to watch his younger brother and sister after school. His parents' divorce was extremely bitter, with Mom

# IMPACT OF DIVORCE ON ACADEMIC ACHIEVEMENT

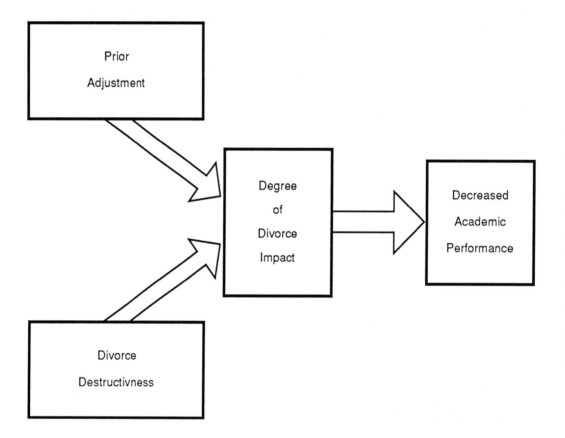

**Figure 1-4** The adolescent's school achievement can be greatly affected by divorce. Poor predivorce adjustment and a destructive divorce can create an impact that disrupts the educational process and the student's ability to learn.

accusing Dad of extramarital affairs and Dad accusing Mom of unnecessary and excessive spending.

The truth of these accusations is really unimportant. Jim was old enough to understand what was going on and the mutual attacks served to alienate him somewhat from both parents. This, combined with his mother's lack of availability (due to work and emotional pain), and separation from his father (due to visits only every other weekend plus father's emotional pain), served to lessen his attachment to both parents at the same time that he lost his peer group and started a new school.

This was a devastating divorce. It resulted in Jim doing very poorly in school. B-C work in seventh and eighth grades became D-F work in high school. He made virtually no friends during his freshman year in school. When he became abusive to his younger brother and sister, his mother finally sought outside counseling for him.

Unfortunately, this story is not unusual. Devastating divorces are common. Frequently, when devastating divorces are combined with poor to low average adjustment, the consequences can be dangerous to the preadolescent and adolescent student. Drug abuse, truancy, promiscuous sexual behavior, attempted suicides, vandalism, and other illegal acting out behaviors are not uncommon.

### Destructive Divorce

In this resource we define a destructive (as opposed to devastating) divorce as one that produces *either* significant environmental change or significant familial change, but not both. The student experiences a profound trauma in one of these two spheres while at the same time receives some support from the other. Note the following examples:

### Case Study—Becky

Becky was fifteen in the summer between her freshman and sophomore years in high school when her parents separated and told her that they were planning a divorce. Her older brother was in his second year in college and already out of the home. Becky's dad had a significant drinking problem. There was considerable blaming between her parents over this problem, and over the issue of her mother's diminishing support of her husband.

The divorce resulted in a terrible ripping apart of the family. Her brother, who had not been around much during the last two years (and consequently was not aware of his dad's recent behavior), being an adult male himself, sided with Becky's father. Becky sided with her mother. The court imposed restrictions on dad's visitation because of his alcohol abuse. She didn't see her father very much, and her brother, whom she had been close to, she saw hardly at all. Her mother was in a constant state of anger and bitterness.

However, because of the length of the marriage and some financial assets, Becky's mom was able to keep the house. Becky remained in the neighborhood and was able to finish her four years of high school with her friends and peers. The support of teachers, friends, and friend's parents proved invaluable to her survival.

### Case Study—David

David, 12 years old and an only child, had just begun seventh grade when his parents divorced. His parents had been growing apart emotionally for years. Their divorce, though sad, was not bitter. David stayed with his mom and saw his dad frequently after school and every other weekend. The divorce forced both his parents to move to less expensive residences. Both parents found apartments in new communities, with mom and David moving closer to mom's work.

The move occurred in the middle of the school year, and the prospect of going to a new school terrified David. However, *both* parents took him for registration and talked with the school administrator about David's fears. They worked together to help David become comfortable. Nevertheless, David's grades dropped sharply that year. It was a difficult transition for him and it was six months before he became comfortable with the transitions in his life. As he made friends and continued to have the support of his family, his adjustment began to improve.

Destructive divorces are also common. Destructive divorces will have a negative impact on self-esteem; consequently, the academic and social performances of students, regardless of their prior adjustment, will be affected. The student's prior adjustment, however, will influence the degree of the negative impact.

### Benevolent Divorce

A "benevolent" divorce produces neither significant environmental change nor significant familial change. Any or all of the seven themes of divorce may still be present for the student, but the impact on self-esteem system will be reduced significantly. If the benevolent divorce occurs for a student who has good or average developmental adjustment, the divorce may have a minimal effect on academic or social performance.

### Case Study—Jenny

Jenny was sixteen and a sophomore in high school when her parents divorced. Her father traveled a lot for his employment. Her parents' divorce, following the initial outburst, was fairly amicable. Jenny stayed with her mother in the townhouse that they had been living in for the last five years. She saw her father every other weekend and sometimes several weekends in a row. She did not sleep at her dad's house or spend the entire weekend, however, because she was socially active and had a part-time job in addition to her academics. Jenny, always close to her mom, actually developed a closer relationship with her father than they had enjoyed in the past. His time with her was limited and both he and Jenny seemed to make the most of it.

Jenny's parents' divorce allowed her to stay at home, remain with her peers at the same school, and keep her part-time job. Her parents did not deprecate each other in front of their daughter and, in fact, supported her attachment to them both. Jenny, whose prior developmental attachment had been average, was not negatively affected by her parents' divorce.

Even the case of the good developmental/benevolent divorce will create some of the described emotional responses. Fear, sense of loss, loneliness, and anger are common in even the most benign divorces. These emotions and the other themes of divorce are exacerbated by the more devastating divorce and poor developmental adjustment.

A student who is lonely, sad, or feeling rejected and angry is going to have a great deal of difficulty coping with the increased academic demands of grades 7 through 12. His or her tolerance for frustration and ability to be empathic to other's feelings will be diminished, therefore affecting his or her ability to meet the new social challenges of adolescence: intimacy, loyalty, dependability, sexuality, and so on.

### Importance of Belonging

Having a sense of feeling part of a family unit is vital for adolescents. One's family provides a stable source of values and reinforcement, of acknowledgment and support for students as they attempt to cope with academic and social tasks. A stable, supportive family unit is preferably provided by the family itself. It can also be provided, however, to a somewhat lesser degree, by a stable, intimate peer group. Because of the destabilizing nature of a divorce, a combination of both family and peer group may be necessary. The family, less stable than before, but supportive, plus an understanding peer group can combine to provide some of the necessary support.

The emotions or themes of divorce, however, are intense. The student's needs are very self-centered. It is unlikely that the "remains" of the family, even with a stable peer group, will be able to meet all the student's needs.

### Meeting Students' Needs With This Program

The program that we have developed and the resulting group process will provide the support, education, and counseling students need to cope with divorce. This group, focused on the divorce trauma, will help provide a sense of family. It will teach the participant new coping skills, help rebuild damaged self-esteem and acknowledge the student's attempts to successfully tackle academic and social challenges. We will guide you through the program and talk about this group process in the next two sections.

Because divorce's effects can be long lasting, the group program presented next can be effective for students whose parents are currently going through a divorce, with those who have been divorced recently, or with those divorced for many years.

*Section 2*

# Establishing and Managing the Group

## ☐ BEGINNING A SUPPORT GROUP

In the process of establishing a support group, you will want to consider the following questions:

▲ Why should a support group be conducted in a school environment?

▲ Who would be an appropriate group leader?

▲ How can you identify students who can benefit from such a group?

▲ How can you interview and invite students to join the group?

▲ How many students—at which levels—should you include in a group?

▲ What scheduling options do you have?

A rationale for conducting a support group in your school is discussed in this section along with answers and optional solutions for these questions and others.

### *Appropriate Settings for Groups*

Traditionally, therapy groups have been offered through hospitals, through private or public-supported mental health facilities, and in connection with religious organizations. All of these settings are appropriate. Lately, however, the school has emerged as a good resource for assisting children from divorced families.

Although some argue that it is not the responsibility of the school to offer psychological services for personal crises, a strong case can be made for the appropriateness of school-based divorce groups. Divorce can, in fact, affect school performance. It has been linked to low self-esteem, decreased ability to concentrate, high absenteeism, and behavioral problems. At the adolescent level, these behavioral problems may include drug and alcohol abuse and early sexual experimentation. The school, because of its stability and regularity, provides organization in the student's life and may serve as a haven from ongoing home conflict. In addition, both children and supportive professionals are already in place in the school, thus reducing the monetary cost of treatment as well as the time investment for the parent.

### Appropriate Group Leaders

Before discussing the steps involved in group establishment, you should give consideration to who should lead the group. In general, the group leader should have well developed basic counseling skills. These would include good listening skills, which would encompass maintaining eye contact and having an "open" posture, attending to the verbal message of the student, and interpreting the student's nonverbal behaviors (such as facial expression, body posture, and tone of voice). The group leader should also have expressive skills such as the ability to convey empathy, to use appropriate probes, and to direct conversation. It is preferable for the group leader to have experience in conducting therapy groups and essential for the leader to have an understanding of psychological group process. Keep in mind that adolescents dealing with divorce issues may be angry or in emotional distress even though there are no overt signs of such feelings. Group therapy may allow them to express these feelings openly. The leader should not only be prepared for this, but should know how to help the adolescent cope with the emerging and sometimes frightening feelings.

In addition to considering group leader qualifications, thought should be given to the amount and type of contact that the leader will have with a student outside of the group setting. It is our opinion that teachers working within the same school as the population to be served are inappropriate group leaders in the junior high and high school settings for the following reasons.

First, the therapy group represents a unique setting that provides both an opportunity for freedom of expression and the security of confidentiality. Group members are encouraged to discuss very personal family issues. They may explore sensitive topics and reveal what they consider to be embarassing information. It is difficult and perhaps unfair for the adolescent to be placed in a situation where he/she must later face the therapist under a different set of circumstances (i.e., the classroom). It can also be a difficult situation for the teacher, who must not allow classroom evaluations to be colored by the personal knowledge that the teacher now has of the student. In addition, the teacher must be careful not to inadvertently reveal information that was shared in confidence.

Second, the student/teacher relationship is quite different from the client/therapist relationship. Within the therapy group, the student is encouraged to actively engage in conversation rather than raise a hand and wait for recognition. Students should be allowed to speak in the manner that they find most comfortable. For many adolescents this includes a liberal array of profanity.

Asking or demanding that the adolescent curtail the use of such language reduces the spontaneity of group participation and the likelihood that a trusting relationship will develop (of the magnitude necessary for the relationship to be truly therapeutic). The teacher who allows such freedoms within the therapy setting may later have difficulty, however, with his/her authority within the classroom as many adolescents have difficulty adapting to fluctuating situational rules. The teacher should simply be aware of this.

A third area of difficulty for the teacher/therapist lies in establishing an appropriate distance between client and therapist. Teachers are more accessible to students than are other service personnel, particularly if a teacher has a group participant in a class they teach. This allows a greater opportunity for a relationship between the client and therapist to develop outside of the group. Students may begin confiding in the teacher outside of group sessions and thus be less likely to share information within the group. The impact of the group experience and of the peer support is reduced, undermining the effectiveness of group therapy. The student may instead become dependent on the teacher. In addition, the teacher may find it difficult to limit the relationship to a therapeutic one, thus reducing therapist objectivity.

Even if the teacher/therapist does not currently have any group members in the classes that he/she is teaching, the structure of the secondary school system is such that it is likely that the student may be in that teacher's class at a future date. The above arguments, or a variation thereof, still hold. Within the school system, then, groups are most appropriately lead by support service personnel such as school psychologists, social workers, school nurse or school counselors, assuming that these individuals have the appropriate skills.

## Checklist for Forming Groups

The following checklist for forming divorce groups will give you an outline of the steps to use in establishing your group. All topics in the checklist will be discussed in this section.

### Identifying Students of Divorce

As students become older, communication between parents and the school tends to break down. That is, it is less likely that parents of secondary school students will officially notify the school of a divorce. There are, however, numerous ways of identifying students in crisis. Many students have a favorite teacher, one in whom they may confide. At the beginning of the school year, send a letter to faculty members outlining the divorce group and ask teachers to be alert to any changes in a student's behavior such as a drop in grades, inattentiveness or excessive daydreaming in class, absenteeism, sadness, or anxiousness which may be indicative of troubles at home. The teacher may then approach the student directly, contact the parent, notify the student's guidance counselor, or contact the school psychologist or social worker. Once the student has been identified as a child of divorce, a referral can be made to the group leader.

# Checklist for Forming Divorce Groups R2-1

1. Identify the students.
    a. Examine school records
    b. Solicit referrals (nurse, teachers, students, counselors)
    c. Send parent newsletters
    d. Visit classes to elicit self-referrals

2. Interview the candidates
    a. Explain the group to the student
    b. Complete the Student Information Form

3. Set up the group
    a. Establish a size—between 6 and 10 students
    b. Meet during the regular school day if possible
    c. Schedule on a rotating basis so that students do not miss the same class repeatedly
    d. Notify teachers of anticipated absences
    e. Send reminders to students for meeting time and place

4. Termination
    a. Decide if the group will meet for 10 sessions or continue beyond the defined sessions.
    b. Explain new parameters should the group continue.

Some students may contact their counselor directly, who may then make a referral to the group leader. The school nurse may also be a source for identifying students. Students whose parents are divorcing may report to the nurse's office with frequent headaches or upset stomachs. Keep in mind that adolescents may be sensitive to issues of confidentiality. That is, after a student confides that his/her parents are divorcing, the student's consent should be obtained before making a referral.

In the schools that have a daily announcement system, the existence of the group may be made known to the student body directly. In others, the group leader may ask teachers to deliver a brief announcement at the beginning of their classes. The group leader may wish to make a personal visit to study halls or physical education classes in order to more fully define the group and answer any questions, giving students the opportunity to refer themselves.

Many schools send a letter to parents at the beginning of the school year or at the begininng of each school semester. An announcement describing the group may be placed in the parent letter. Parents should be urged to contact the group leader and identify their children as possible candidates for inclusion in the divorce group.

The family background of all transferees should be examined to determine if there has been a divorce in the student's immediate family history. Frequently, a divorce or remarriage initiates a family move. These adolescents are especially vulnerable because they have not only experienced familial changes, but peer group changes as well. Each school should adopt a transfer form that identifies individuals from divorced families. Students should then be referred to the group leader.

When the student is enrolled in the school, the parent typically completes a form identifying the legal guardian. When the records do not specifically identify the parents as being divorced, the marital status may be inferred from the guardianship. If the guardian is listed as a single individual (single parent), or the last name of the guardians differs from that of the student (step-parents), that student may be from a divorced family. Obviously this is not a fail-safe system, however, and the only way to confirm the assumption is to ask the student.

### Which Students Should Be Invited to Participate?

Group inclusion should not be limited to students whose parents are in the midst of divorce. Problems rooted in a divorce that occurred during the adolescent's early years may persist, may reappear, or may appear for the first time years after the divorce separation has occurred. In addition, many students continue to live in the shadow of the parents' never-ending conflicts. Disputes that preceded the divorce often remain unsolved and continue to be issues of contention. Other conflicts may center on custody and visitation issues or disputes arising due to parental inability to adjust to the divorce. If a parent remarries, the adolescent must learn to cope with the difficulties arising from inclusion in a step-family. Adolescents in high conflict situations may be subject to lowered self-esteem, high anxiety, feelings of loss of control, grief, and depression. Students whose parents are divorced may be identified from school records.

One other issue that is often debated when deciding whom to include in treatment groups, is that of participant suitability. That is, should individuals who are known to be drug abusers, or have police records, or have been hospitalized for mental health reasons, or have any other "questionable" traits, be included in the treatment group? It should be kept in mind that adolescents from divorced families are likely to be dually diagnosed. These individuals come from dysfunctional families. They may have parents who are alcoholics, drug addicts, or who are mentally ill. Students who are suicidal or are potentially dangerous to themselves or others should be referred to an outside agency for treatment. All others should be considered potential group participants.

### Student Interview

Each student should be contacted individually and invited to participate. The group purpose should be outlined and the meeting schedule explained. It is important to emphasize that participation in the group is voluntary and that everything to be discussed within the group is confidential. If the student expresses an interest in participating in the group, an initial interview should be conducted. Collect basic information about the student. For example, the student's age and year in school, age at the time of the divorce, who the student is living with, and any other information that may help in understanding the student's current situational needs. Refer to the sample Student Identification Form that follows. This form will be used for your ongoing group evaluation (to be discussed later). Information may be added at any time and you should strive to keep these records current.

Depending on the school's policy or on state regulations, parental consent to participate in the group may or may not be required. Groups offered on a regular basis may be considered to be a part of the curriculum and parental consent would therefore not be required. A bulletin in the parent newsletter stating that the groups will be offered to all interested students together with a phone number that concerned parents may call for further information may suffice. If parental consent is needed, the student should be informed that his/her parents will be contacted. This is an important point because many adolescents will not want their parents to know that they wish to participate in a therapy group. A suitable sample letter to parents is provided on page 51.

### Number and Age Range of Participants

Ideally, groups should consist of eight students no more than two years apart in age. Groups that are too small do not develop the appropriate group dynamics and are especially vulnerable to member absences. In groups that are too large, there is a tendency for subgroups to form, making it hard to focus group attention on a single topic and undermining group cohesion. In addition, as the group gets

# STUDENT IDENTIFICATION FORM R2-2

## (Instructor's Sheet)

Student's name: _____

Year in school: _____

Birthdate: _____ Age: _____

Number of years in this school: _____

Has student participated in prior groups at this school? _____

Has student participated in other divorce groups? _____ Where? ___

_____

Date of initial interview _____

Date of entry into group _____

Notes _____

_____

_____

_____

_____

Student's age at time of parents' separation: _____

Student's age at time of parents' divorce: _____

Siblings:

    age: _____ sex: _____ male _____ female _____

    age: _____ sex: _____ male _____ female _____

    age: _____ sex: _____ male _____ female _____

With which parent does student live? _____ mother _____ father

Are all siblings living together? _____ yes _____ no

If no, with whom do they live? _____

_____

_____

# STUDENT IDENTIFICATION FORM R2-2 (cont'd)
## (Instructor's Sheet)

How did the student find out about the group?

    A)   Student referral    _____

    B)   Teacher referral    _____

    C)   Counselor referral   _____

    D)   Other   _____

| | | |
|---|---|---|
| Does the student live with a stepparent? | yes | no |
| Does the student live with a stepsibling? | yes | no |
| Does the student live with half-siblings? | yes | no |
| Does the student visit the noncustodial parent? | yes | no |
| Is there a stepparent present during visitation? | yes | no |
| Are there stepsiblings present during visitation? | yes | no |
| Are there half-siblings present during visitation? | yes | no |

Notes: _____

_____

_____

_____

_____

_____

# LETTER TO PARENTS R2-3

SUBURBAN HIGH SCHOOL
STREET ADDRESS
TOWN, STATE, ZIP
PHONE NUMBER

Dear Parent,

This fall Suburban High School will be offering several support groups for students who are living in single-parent or stepparent families as a result of parental divorce. The groups, utilizing a discussion format, provide an opportunity for teens to meet with other individuals who have had similar experiences. Your son/daughter has been invited to participate in one of these groups.

Groups will meet once a week for 10 weeks during the regular school day. Each weekly session will focus on a topic of interest to adolescents, for instance, issues such as building self-confidence or developing interpersonal relationships. These adult-guided peer support groups offer students the opportunity to explore and express their thoughts and feelings.

We at Suburban High School are looking forward to a successful year and anticipate a great deal of student involvement. If you have any questions regarding the program, please feel free to contact me through the school guidance office (phone number).

Sincerely,

_____

larger, there is less time available for each individual. The acceptable group size ranges between six and ten students.

Because adolescents are maturing both cognitively and socially, group members should be fairly close together in age. We have on occasion, however, successfully conducted groups with participants ranging in age from high school freshman to high school senior. In those cases, during the early stages of group development, we found it necessary to give additional support to the younger members so that they were not overwhelmed by the older members.

Keep in mind, also, that students will respond to some concepts based on their level of cognitive development and maturity. Students who vary in age may have different concerns. For example, seniors may hold jobs, drive a car, and plan to go away to college. This makes them considerably less dependent on their parents than freshmen are; thus, the concerns of each age group are markedly different.

### Scheduling the Groups

Group sessions should be conducted on a weekly basis. Although some schools prefer that support groups be held before or after school, we believe that groups should be conducted during the regular school day. It is difficult to get students to participate in groups outside of school hours. There may be conflicts with bus schedules, athletic events, or school social functions. Older students may have jobs. One of the following approaches may help.

1. Schedule groups during study halls. This may limit the population can be served since many students do not have study halls.

2. Schedule a "brown bag" lunch group. Students are invited to bring their lunches to the group session. Although this is far from our first choice option, we have found this to be a workable idea at the upper high school level. Junior high students, however, tend to have difficulty mustering the maturity necessary for such functions.

3. Schedule the group on a rotating basis. That is, the group may meet during the first period of the day for the first session, the second period of the day for the second session, and so on through as many periods as desired. We typically rotate scheduling through five periods. Students then miss only two classes, five weeks apart, of any given subject. Teachers should be informed that the student will be absent from their class on the scheduled date.

Keep in mind that student confidentiality must be maintained. Do not discuss the reason that the student is being included in a group with anyone. See the sample Teacher Notification Form that follows.

It may be helpful to send students a reminder notice on the day of the scheduled group meeting. Tell them where to meet if there is not a fixed meeting location, and what period of the day has been scheduled for that week. We always instruct students to report to the group session directly and not go to their

# TEACHER NOTIFICATION FORM R2-4

Date: _____

To:

From:

The following students will be participating in a support group formed by the guidance department. The group will meet once a week, for ten weeks, for an entire class period. The scheduled time will rotate through five class periods. Students will be told that they are expected to make up any missed work whenever possible, and that they should report to the classroom on days when exams are scheduled. If you have any questions, please contact the school guidance office.

| Student Name | Period to be Missed | Date |
| --- | --- | --- |
| _____ | _____ | _____ |
| _____ | _____ | _____ |
| _____ | _____ | _____ |
| _____ | _____ | _____ |
| _____ | _____ | _____ |

classroom first as this delays the group when students straggle in at different times.

### Topical Approach to Sessions

The sessions in the Treatment Program are topical. That is, there is a suggested issue to be discussed at each session. This format is intended to establish the breadth and scope of the group. It also provides a point of common experience with which to begin discussions. Younger group members may also need the structure afforded by planned activities because they lack the appropriate skills. Handouts are available and activities are suggested for inclusion in the younger groups. The topical approach, however, keeps the group dependent on the leader. It makes it more difficult to move the group into the working stage. The group progresses through the material faster and moves through the initial stage more rapidly, but it does not develop the depth that a more member-controlled group could develop. For this reason, each session begins with free discussion. Ask if anything of interest has happened in the past week or if anyone wants to discuss something that is important to them. The sessions are not intended to be used rigidly. When an appropriate topic is brought up by a student, the leader should encourage the group to pursue it until the topic is exhausted.

The time available to the group should determine how flexible the program should be. If only the minimal ten sessions are available, it is best to stick to the sessions as planned. But if a semester or a whole year is available, then the group can be very flexible. You can then allow the group more than one session to work through a topic. The important thing is to cover all of the material.

### Termination or Continuation?

The tenth session addresses issues of termination. If your time constraints are such that you cannot continue with the group sessions, then follow the suggestions outlined in the termination session. We typically do not terminate at this time. The ten-session program was intended to be a starting point for building self-esteem, developing coping skills, and providing information about divorce and divorce issues. The program was designed, though, as a short-term intervention and termination is possible at this point. Allowing students to continue to meet as a group increases the likelihood that the presented material will be internalized. The ten-session program then serves to establish the scope and function of the group.

At the end of the ten-week period, you will find that group cohesion, trust, and mutual respect are well established. Groups may begin to meet on a two week cycle. That is, the group would meet every other week instead of weekly. The same period rotation pattern would apply. It has been our experience that well established groups do not need a curriculum. Students will, by this time, recognize the group as a place to discuss personal problems. It is your job, as the leader, to keep the group focused within the already established parameters, but allow the students to dictate the topic. Groups may run for a semester or for the entire year.

### Adding Students to an Established Group

Introducing new students to a group that has been meeting for only a few sessions alters the group dynamics and delays the development of trust and group cohesion. Adding new students to a group that is halfway through the program probably has little benefit for the new member if the group will terminate after the tenth session. If, however, the group continues to meet (even on a less frequent basis), it is possible to add students to an established group.

The group members should be informed that a new member will be joining them at the following session. Do not disclose the identity of the new student as this is a violation of the student's privacy (especially should he/she decide not to join the group at the last moment). The group members should be allowed a few moments to discuss the impact of the new member. With junior high and high school students it is highly unlikely that there will be any objections to a new member.

The new member should be introduced at the first session that he/she attends. Some individuals may feel uncomfortable being the "new" person, so it is wise to let the person be an "observer" during the first few sessions. If he/she does not start to participate after that, encourage him/her to do so by asking questions or by directing other members' conversations toward the new member. Although the new person will not have the benefit of the formal instruction provided in the early sessions, many of the early issues will be spontaneously readdressed and the new member will benefit from the new discussion.

It is also possible to combine students from different groups as they complete the ten-week program. At the end of the ten-week program, some students will elect not to continue. Those students who wish to continue may do so as a smaller group. As a second group finishes the program, some members will again elect to continue. At this point, the two groups of continuing members may be combined.

You should always discuss such changes with group members before implementing them. Be sure to ask if there are any objections. We have found that junior high and high school students operate on a "more the merrier" basis. We have never encountered objections to combining groups at this stage. Combining groups does, however, affect group cohesion and it may take a few sessions to reestablish trust and group cohesion.

Students in continuously running groups will self-terminate. That is, as they reach the point where they feel that they are no longer deriving benefit from group participation, they will announce their intent to leave. This should be discussed in the group to prepare the remaining members for the change in dynamics. At the time of this writing, one author has been leading a group that was established four years ago and has maintained a relatively constant size (9-10 students) although only three of the original members remain.

## ☐ GROUP THEORY

In some ways, a therapy group is like a giant interpersonal relationship. It changes, grows, and develops based upon the mutual experiences of its members and each individual's perceptions of those experiences. Like any newly developing friendship, the group passes through various stages of development. The rate at which the group progresses is influenced by such things as the developmental level of the participants, the amount of structure imposed on the group, and the amount and type of leader intervention. Although many stages and substages have been identified, we will discuss only the four basic stages of group development.

## ☐ INITIAL STAGE

### Participant Fears

The initial stage, lasting from three to six sessions, is characterized by a high degree of tension. Most adolescents view the initial sessions as a threatening situation. They are uncertain about what might "happen to them" and are unclear about what is expected. In addition, most adolescents are extremely concerned about their own self-image. They have a strong desire to make a good impression, both on the group leader and on the other members of the group. Because the other members are unfamiliar to them, they hesitate to participate for fear of embarrassing themselves. Students in the educational system have learned that teachers may call on them when they are unprepared. Hence, there is a distrust of the leader (who is often viewed initially as a teacher), again, for fear of possible embarrassment. Even though each student has volunteered or perhaps requested to be a part of the group, during the initial sessions, participating in the group long-term will require the sharing of personal information. Thus, students risk damage to their egos if they are rejected or ridiculed by the other group members. There is also a certain amount of distrust of the other group members. That is, each individual fears that what he says in the group may be taken out of the group by other members. The group as a whole is, paradoxically, *resistant* to the therapy process.

### Resistance

Therapeutic resistance is a reluctance on the part of the patient or the group as a whole to participate in the treatment process. In the early stages of group development, resistance may be attributed to the immmediate fears evoked by being in an unfamiliar setting. It can be thought of as a *fear of the unknown*. In a group like this, the student may have to face some difficult or painful issues. In this case, resistance also arises through the confrontations of those issues.

Fear-based resistance may be manifested as silence or defensive body posturing. It is likely that when you begin the first group session, you will find most of the participants deeply engrossed in studying the carpet! It is during these introductory sessions that you will be most directive. You must understand what to expect in terms of group process and have a "game plan" or strategy for running the group. Without this strategy the group will fail.

During the first session, discuss the rationale for participating in a therapy group. You should clearly define and establish the rules for the group. You should begin to establish expectations for member participation. This is not as easy as it sounds. In the first sessions, group cohesiveness will be extremely low. That is, group members may be reluctant to talk much to each other. Rather, they will address their comments to the leader or may remain silent. It is the silence that most group leaders, as well as the participants, find disturbing.

It is important to keep in mind that *silence is a manifestation of resistance.* As such, it is a normal part of the group experience. Whenever group members are uncomfortable, there will be resistance. A reasonable amount of resistance is to be expected if you are doing your job. If there is too much resistance, however, the group will not be able to function.

In the early stages of group development, it is your job to help the group work through the resistance so that it can move forward. If you as the leader are too authoritarian, you will set yourself apart from the group, creating an "us against them" situation. If you give them too much direction, they will become permanently dependent on you, and thus slow the progress through the different stages. Too little direction will stall the group in the early developmental stage.

### Content Versus Process

One way of controlling the amount of stress in a group, and thus the amount of resistance, is to know when to focus on the content of the discussion and when to focus on the processes that are taking place at any given moment within the group. *Content refers to the actual words or information that is discussed by group members.* For example, if a group member is relaying a day at school, the description of the day's events would be content. *Process refers to the reactions and interactions that occur within the group as a whole or between the group members.* This refers not to the words that are being spoken between individuals, but instead the motives behind those words. Why are the words spoken at this particular time? Suppose an individual began talking about school as a means of changing the subject to one that he/she considered safe. The fact that the individual changed the subject as a means of avoiding an unpleasant topic is the *process.*

You may choose to focus on the content of the message (by allowing the person to describe a day at school) or focus on the process by which the person changed the subject (by noting to the individual and the group members that the topic of conversation has been turned away from a potentially painful experience). Process can also include nonverbal messages:

▲ Where do students sit within the group?
▲ How do the listeners respond to the speaker?
▲ Are students silent or do they stare at the floor?

Process reveals information about individual personalities and about the interpersonal relationships between the group participants. Commenting on process is a comment on behavior.

A therapy group is a microcosm. What occurs within the group most likely occurs outside the group. For example, the student who alienates the other participants probably has trouble making friends outside the group. Topics that are avoided in group sessions are most likely painful and are not dealt with outside of the group. Keep in mind that the processes that occur within the group are representative of the processes of everyday life. Focusing on the processes that occur within the group will help students to recognize and work through similar processes in their personal lives.

In general, focusing on the content is less anxiety provoking than focusing on process. In the early sessions, you will probably need to focus more on content. Students are encouraged to present content information about themselves. That is, members are asked to introduce themselves and share some personal, but nonthreatening, information about themselves such as their age, their year in school, and hobbies or job status. You may focus on content by asking for more detail. For example, if a student reveals that she plays tennis, you may ask how long she has been playing or if she is on a tennis team outside of the school setting. Another way to focus on content is to make *clarification statements*. That is, paraphrase what the individual has just said. Clarification statements do not have any evaluative quality to them. It should be noted that the type of content information shared with the group in the early stages is basically "common knowledge" information. That is, participants tend to share superficial nonthreatening information.

Process commentary creates anxiety because, as already noted, it is a comment on behavior. Commenting on behavior can make people self-conscious. Process commentary can also force the group to deal with a topic that it is trying to avoid. In the initial stage of group development, this is counterproductive. It increases resistance and decreases the rate at which group cohesion is developed.

It is best to avoid most process commentary until the group reaches a more advanced stage. There is one case, however, in which process commentary can reduce anxiety and help the group work through resistance. For example, you may make a comment about the apparent anxiety of the group members. You can then hypothesize as to why this is. For example, "I've noticed that people are shifting in their seats and staring at the floor. Maybe you're uncomfortable because you don't know what you're supposed to do."

You may also incorporate *universalizing statements* into the observation as a means of further reducing the anxiety. A universalizing statement takes the focus off a single individual by applying the statement to the group in general. For example, "I see that people are feeling anxious. Most people are anxious during the first few sessions because they don't know each other and they don't know what they are supposed to do." You're acknowledging the behavior and normalizing the feeling by saying that everyone feels the same way.

You, as the leader, must learn to provide enough direction to keep the group moving forward in its development without creating a dependency. It is not your job to entertain the group members nor to rescue them from uncomfortable silences. You should strive towards establishing a group that runs itself. That is, the group should be cohesive and self-reliant. *Cohesion occurs when members recognize each individual as a part of the group and work together to attain each person's goals. The group is self-reliant when the group members "own" the therapy process and actively participate in it.* This must occur if they are to derive any benefit from the treatment. Too much leader control will reduce participant ownership.

### Respect and Genuineness

Leadership style and competency have a great deal to do with creating a successful group (one that runs itself). Perhaps the most important element of leadership is attitude. Yalom (1985) identified two very important elements of attitude; *respect* and *genuineness*. *Respect implies that the individuals are valued as human beings.* They should be acknowledged as having their own unique qualities without critical judgement on the part of the therapist. Respect can be communicated in a variety of ways. For example, listening attentively when a group member talks, expressing warmth and empathy (communicating a basic understanding of what is being said), and providing appropriate reinforcement.

*Genuineness refers to being oneself.* There should be no facade. Genuine leaders don't say things they don't mean. They do not offer phoney, "pat" answers or pretend to be compassionate. Teenagers are very quick to identify someone who is misrepresenting themselves. Should they feel that you are being phoney or dishonest, the group will fail even before it starts. As a rule of thumb, "don't say it if you don't mean it." Be spontaneous and open. Be willing to self-disclose when appropriate. A genuine leader is not threatened when a group member challenges him/her. Criticism should not be taken personally. Rather, as genuine leader, you should attempt to understand why the group member feels the way he/she does. It is essential that you exhibit these two qualities, particularly during the early group sessions.

### Speaking and Active Listening

Being a good communicator involves both speaking (with one's voice and body) and being a good listener. You should strive towards modeling appropriate speaking skills as well as active listening skills. In the early stages of group development, members usually do not speak to one another directly. Instead, they tend to speak to the group leader or to the floor. This behavior indicates that group members have not yet developed the speaking skills and the active listening skills that come with time and practice.

### Arranging the Room

There are ways of structuring the setting to facilitate positive communication. Ideally, the group sessions should be conducted in a room that allows for the formation of an eight- to ten-foot diameter circle. The chairs should be arranged around the perimeter of the circle. A reasonably upright chair without arms can facilitate an open posture which, on the part of the speaker, communicates a willingness to engage in a verbal exchange. That is, it invites a response from the listeners. School books should be left outside of the room or stored under the students' chairs. The room should not have a center table. Books and tables provide an effective barrier for the group participants. Hands should be free of objects which may be played with unconsciously, such as pencils, erasers, and so forth. These objects may distract the speaker's audience.

### Qualities of a Good Speaker

An effective speaker faces the listening audience and works to maintain eye contact with them. This tells the listener that the speaker is monitoring the audience and is genuinely interested in delivering some message. Eye contact also personalizes the speaker's involvement with each individual listener. You should meet each individual's eyes while speaking and should direct the group members to do the same.

Voice control is also important for a speaker. You should try to maintain an even speech tempo and not become too loud. A quiet voice conveys patience and control. Raising your voice suggests that you believe only your opinion is correct and that you are not willing to hear the other side of the story. Loud voices can be punitive, thus decreasing the likelihood that communication will continue. There are also gestures that can cut off communication. For example, pointing or wagging your finger is aggressive and offensive to the receiver. As an effective speaker, you must monitor both your speech and gestures.

### Qualities of a Good Listener

Being a good listener is an important part of being a good communicator. A good listener is an *active listener*. Active listeners adopt an open posture. That is, your arms and legs should not be crossed, as this may communicate defensiveness. An open posture communicates a willingness to be with the speaker. An active listener faces the individual who is speaking. A body that is half turned away, such as through sitting sideways on a chair that is facing forward, suggests to the listener that you are not particularly interested in what he has to say.

Good eye contact, that is, looking directly at the person who is speaking, tells the person that you are involved in what he is saying, and want to hear what he has to say. As previously noted, you may find that in the initial sessions of the therapy group, many of the members will stare at the floor. This should tell you that they are unwilling to engage in conversation, or at least that they are uncomfortable about it. Some participants may be willing to look at you, but their eyes may dart away when you look at them directly. Disengaging eye contact is a way of hiding. The unconscious message is that if I can't see you, then you can't see me.

Certain other bodily gestures on the part of the listener can also facilitate communication. For example, leaning slightly toward a speaker during an intense discussion tells the speaker that you are listening attentively and following what is being said. Smiling or nodding one's head communicates not only agreement, but also that you understand what the speaker is saying. You should always strive to be an active listener.

Active listening involves listening to both the verbal and the nonverbal message that the speaker is sending. The verbal message may consist of a description of an event such as a date or trip, a description of behavior such as fighting, or the expression of an emotion, such as anger.

An active listener not only listens to the content of the message but also notes patterns or themes that keep recurring. For example, you might notice the number of times that a student describes being involved in fights. The verbal message may include an implied message or an inference. You need to be aware of what is not said as well as what is stated directly.

A good listener should be able to interpret gestures and body movements; facial expressions such as smiles, frowns, pursed lips and nervous twitches; voice quality such as changes in pitch or loudness; voice inflection, speed, fluency, and silences; autonomic responses, such as blushing, shortness of breath, or sweating; and the person's style and manner of dress, neatness, and overall appearance. You should also note whether or not the nonverbal behavior is consistent with what the person is saying verbally. You may use these observations to focus the group's attention on the processes occurring within the group or as a means of redirecting the conversation and challenging the thought processes of a single individual.

## ☐ MIDDLE STAGE

The middle stage of group development usually starts to appear between the third and sixth group session. Some of the unknown factors have been removed. The participants are now clear about what is expected of them. They have a fairly good idea of what the group is about and how the session will progress. This knowledge provides a certain amount of security and serves to reduce the anxiety level. In addition, as the individuals become more familiar with the other group members, trust begins to develop, which serves to further reduce the group tension. As the tension is reduced, group participation begins to increase.

Although there is a topic outlined for each session, it is important that you begin each session with an open discussion. Ask members if there is anything that they wish to discuss during the group session. In the early sessions of the middle stage, be prepared for potential silence at the beginning of each session. It is important to let the group work through this silence. That is, wait for a *group member* to begin the discussion. In this way, the group members begin to take control of the therapeutic process.

Initially, the topics participants will bring up for discussion will be fairly neutral. Individuals may talk about things heard on the news, about sports teams, or about school-related activities. At this point, all of the above topics would be acceptable. There is one topic, however, that is highly likely to surface, yet is unacceptable: Group members may try to take the focus off of themselves by discussing individuals who are not a part of the working group. Do not allow them to do this. Caution group members that they may not discuss problems or activities of persons who are not a part of the group, or who are group members but are not present.

As each session passes, member participation will increase. The topics chosen for the initial discussion will become more personal and presented more honestly as each individual's anxiety level decreases.

With the individual's reduction in anxiety, resistance to the therapeutic process begins to decrease. But resistance of the group as a whole is likely to remain high. That is, individual members begin to lose their fear of rejection and become more confident in their own ability to participate in the process. The group, however, cannot yet function as a cohesive unit. The members' individual personalities begin to emerge as group members explore their positions within the group.

Some individuals may begin to align themselves with other group members, forming subgroups within the larger group. As this occurs, individuals may begin to engage in private conversations. It is your responsibility as the leader to disallow this. Private conversations should be redirected to the group as a whole.

Power struggles may also surface within the group. More assertive group members may struggle amongst themselves to assume leadership roles. While people's innate personalities will, to a certain degree, dictate the roles that each member will ultimately play within the group, it is the responsibility of the leader to make sure that all group members get equal time.

As the group struggles to reach an equilibrium, the group members will frequently change the subject to nonrelated tasks. You should reinforce the time that the group spends on task. Bear in mind, though, that changing the topic is a defensive maneuver to reduce tension.

You cannot and should not attempt to force the group to remain on task 100 percent of the time. You might use process commentary to redirect the group to the original topic. For example, you may make a comment to the group saying that you have noticed that the subject has changed. You can then ask the group why they think this has happened.

### Empathizing and Clarifying

It is during the middle sessions that you should focus on the group process. It is during this time that you are most likely to be challenged by group members. You should meet these challenges by turning them back to the group for discussion. That is, challenges should be dealt with on a process level and not on a content level. Your role at this time should be nonconfrontational. You should concentrate on expressing empathy through the use of active listening skills. Individuals' statements should be reiterated in a manner that may clarify and/or summarize what has already been said. You should refrain from making interpretations or offering advice while group resistance remains fairly high.

### Transference

With each session during the middle stage, the anxiety level continues to fall. Resistance also is reduced with the passage of time. The group moves towards becoming a cohesive unit. As this happens, transference begins to occur. *Transference is defined as the displacement of thoughts and feelings from one person to another.* For example, let's suppose that a group member has an angry exchange with the football coach. The student then comes to group and displays anger towards the group leader. This anger was unprovoked and unjustified. The student has transferred his anger to another adult authority figure.

Transference may be either positive or negative. That is, a group member may express unrealistic affection towards the group leader as well as unrealistic anger. Too much positive transfer can create resistance because the individual will try to please the therapist. Too much negative transfer causes the individual to become defensive and uncooperative. Transference is thought to occur because the group leader remains somewhat of an ambiguous figure. Individuals will impose organization onto an ambiguous stimulus so that it will fit within their perceptions of reality. In some cases, individuals will respond to the therapist or group leader as they would to other people in their lives who may have similar traits or characteristics.

Transference occurs in all therapeutic relationships. At the moment of its occurrence, the transference is unconscious. Transference may, however, increase the student's resistance to the therapeutic process. If the resistance increases to such a degree that it impedes the student's progress, you may wish to point out the transference to the student.

In some cases the transference is just below the individual's awareness. If this is true, then calling attention to the transference will cause it to come into the student's conscious awareness. In other cases, the transference is deeply unconscious. If you attempt to bring it to the conscious awareness of the student, the student will most likely deny it, resulting in hostility and an even greater increase in resistance.

### Confronting the Belief System

As time passes, the group resistance begins to fall. Assuming that individual resistance remains low, and the group members now perceive themselves as a cohesive unit, the group can now be considered a working group. At this point, you should be spending a minimum amount of time on directing group activities. Your responses to group members can move from clarifying statements to confrontational statements. *A confrontational statement is one which challenges a person's belief system.*

It is not the leader's role to confront the *individual,* but rather to confront the *material.* Suppose a group member denies feeling any hostility toward his father who, at best, is inconsistent with visitation. Yet, whenever he discusses his father, he displays physiological signs of anger. The person is clearly denying the feeling of anger unconsciously. As the leader, you could challenge the belief of not feeling anger by noting the physical changes that occur the next time he talks about his father. For example: "I've noticed that lately when you talk about your father, your voice becomes very loud and your speech becomes more rapid and agitated. What are you feeling right now?"

### Interpretive Statements

Once the group reaches this working stage of development, you are free to provide insight and make interpretive statements. *An interpretive statement addresses the underlying message or unspoken motive.* It serves to focus attention on feelings and can bring subconscious thoughts into conscious awareness. For example, suppose a group member describes her stepmother in the following way:

"My stepmother is such a bitch. She's always on my case and she butts in when I'm trying to talk to my dad."

You may respond by saying, "So you're angry with your stepmother because you feel she doesn't allow you to have private time with your dad."

### Defenses

Many of your interpretations will focus on the individual's or the group's defenses. We all employ various defenses such as denial and projection to keep our egos intact and protect our personal belief system. Defenses protect us from painful situations. Sometimes, however, defenses can get in the way of working through painful experiences so that change and growth cannot occur. It is necessary, then, to challenge those defenses by bringing them into conscious awareness.

As the group moves further into this working stage, the emphasis should shift from process back to content. The material presented at this time should be honest, sincere, and highly personal. It is appropriate at this time to pursue content on a deeper level. That is, you should help the individual explore underlying feelings and ideas, not the superficial details.

### Intense Sessions

Once the group reaches this level of functioning, there will be fluctuations in the intensity of the sessions from week to week. The group will most likely not pick up where they left off the previous week. This is normal. If a group has a very intense session one week, the following session will most likely be more superficial. Intensity tends to scare people. The individuals' resistance will increase. The resistance must fall before the group can proceed.

During intense sessions, students may tend to open themselves too quickly. That is, they may disclose extremely personal information before they are really ready to share it or to deal with the consequences of such disclosures. The student's anxiety level may rise sharply because such disclosures make people feel vulnerable. This may cause the student to quit the group abruptly in order to escape the fearful feelings brought on by feeling vulnerable. You should pace such disclosures so as to protect the student. One way of pacing disclosures is to move the focus off a single individual by asking the group members to share similar experiences.

# ☐ TERMINATION STAGE

Terminating the group is important. As noted previously, the group is a microcosm of life. There are many things in life that have beginnings, middles, and endings. The termination stage is much like graduating from high school, or watching a close friend move away, or even dealing with the death of a loved one. There is much to be learned from this stage of group development.

In a long-running group, one that has continued for one or two semesters, termination begins three to four weeks before the final session. The leader should review presented material and encourage the further development of newly acquired skills. The progress and achievements of the group should be discussed. Everyone must first deal with the event cognitively.

Ending the group also creates an emotional loss. Students may have formed bonds that will be painful to break. They have shared very intimate parts of their lives. For many, it has been the first time that they have experienced such intimate relationships. You, as the leader, should model the sharing of feelings of intimacy. For example, you may select a favorite characteristic of each individual and tell them how or why you will miss them and their special trait.

The group members will also be dealing with feelings of loss — loss of friendships and loss of the support that the group has provided. You should focus group discussion on these feelings, perhaps by asking each person, in turn, to share his/her feelings of loss with the group. The discussion of feelings will allow people to normalize those feelings and begin disengaging from the group. As a final exercise, you may ask the group members to share one thing that they have learned and one memory that they will take away with them.

*Section 3*

# Treatment Program: A Ten-Session Guide

The following pages contain instructions for conducting a ten-session support group for adolescents from divorced families. Although the sessions are complete, the leader is not required, nor expected, to stick to the presented text rigidly. The minilectures are presented as examples only. The activities may be interchanged with other activities that the leader is comfortable with so long as the integrity of the program is not altered. It may, in fact, be necessary to adjust the difficulty of some of the material to compensate for the varying age levels of the participants. Also, it is not necessary to complete all of the material allotted for one session. Material may be carried over into the next session. Most importantly, the leader should be sensitive to the needs of the group. It is more important to deal with immediate crises than to cover the material intended for a particular session. Material skipped during one session can be worked into another session, or an extra session can be added. Be a flexible leader!

# ☐ SESSION ONE:   Introduction and Rationale for Group Participation

### Goals:

*1.* To explain the purpose of the group and how the group will function.

*2.* To introduce group members to one another.

*3.* To administer the self-competency scale.

### Strategy:

*1.* Introduce the group leader.

*2.* Have group members introduce themselves.

*3.* Explain the importance of discussion.

*4.* Explain the use of the various materials.

*5.* Allow the group to discuss individual divorce experiences.

*6.* Administer the self-competency scale.

### Rationale:

Begin the session with introductions. Include a few self-disclosure statements as a model for self-disclosure and to establish a more personal tone for the group (thus eliminating the "classroom" atmosphere). These statements should be rather general. Perhaps note how long you have been employed at your present job, where you went to college, and so forth. Group members should then identify themselves. Encourage them to share some kind of personal information, such as special interests or hobbies to facilitate future self-disclosure and establish a conversational atmosphere. You should then explain the format of the group to establish the framework in which the participants will function.

To provide a cognitive framework for understanding why support groups are effective, explain why group discussion is helpful. The groups are designed to be interactive, so present all information to the participants directly—in the form of minilectures or otherwise—in a manner that invites student participation. For example, ask students why they feel group discussion might be effective and then weave those ideas into the material to be presented. This promotes a sense of group involvement and student control of the group. (Each session outline prompts you to do this by suggesting questions.)

As a first step to developing group cohesion, ask students to share their divorce experiences with the group. You should ask content questions—details about specific divorce events—as a means of expressing interest in each individual. This also allows group members to compare experiences and find commonalities as a means of normalizing the experience. As the group leader, you should try to reflect the emotions that are expressed while each individual describes his/her experience as a first step toward identifying and learning to express the feelings associated with divorce. Administer the self-competency scale in preparation for the following session. The steps that follow provide directions, in outline format, for conducting the group session.

## STEPS:

I. The leader introduces him/herself.

He/She should include a brief personal statement. *Ask each student, in turn, to introduce themselves.* Each person should give their name and offer a short statement about themselves.

II. Briefly outline the format of the group for the participants. Explain that the materials used will include short readings, and questionnaires/surveys. The readings will be used to convey specific information, illustrate concepts, and stimulate discussion. The questionnaires / surveys will be used to provide personal insight for group members and to evaluate group effectiveness.

III. Allow 15 minutes to administer the self-competency scale.

Explain that it is an example of what a survey is like. Tell the participants that it will be used in next week's group session.

IV. Explain why discussion is useful.

A. Tell them that the group is not necessarily for individuals with problems. It is a place where people can discuss the kinds of feelings, ideas, and questions that normally occur when parents separate or divorce.

B. *Ask the group to generate ideas about why talking may be useful.* The ideas should basically relay the following:

▲ Talking allows comparison of ideas and feelings. We all like to compare ourselves to others; to know that we are not alone in our experiences. (This normalizes our experience.)

▲ Talking helps organize our thoughts.

▲ Talking/discussion allows for *brainstorming.* New ideas or solutions to problems may be generated. When we have a choice as to how we deal with problems, it provides a sense of control.

▲ Talking allows for expression of things that would normally be repressed. (Do not dwell on this issue as it will be discussed later.)

### Sample minilecture:

Ninety percent of adults get professional help; they seek someone to talk to who is knowledgeable about divorce. Yet 25 percent or fewer children of divorce receive any outside help.

*Ask students how many got counseling. Ask about support from family or friends.*

Many students report that they did not receive support from family members. Although they may have confided in a friend, many people feel that the friends didn't really understand unless they had also experienced divorce. The purpose of this group is to provide information about divorce and to offer the opportunity to talk to other students who have had similar experiences.

**V.** Explain the Group Rules.

    A. *Rule of Confidentiality.* What is discussed in the group stays within the group. Group members should not repeat what others have said during the session. Members should respect the trust of others.

    B. *Right to Pass.* Participants do not have to reveal information they do not wish to share with the group. Individual privacy will be respected.

**VI.** *Ask each participant, in turn, to briefly describe their divorce experience.* As each student talks, ask questions that demonstrate an interest in what they are saying and convey the idea that you are listening. This may be done by asking for clarification of details or asking for additional content information. In addition, if the student is expressing a strong emotion, reflect the feeling back to him/her ("sounds to me like you were really angry"). Do not, however, dwell on the emotional element. Focus on content. Emotions will be dealt with later. Ask if others have had similar experiences ("Does anyone else have an alcoholic parent?") or point out experiences that are similar ("Abe, your situation sounds similar to Bart's"). Encourage other group members to ask questions and participate in the discussion. Do not spend too much time on a single individual, however. Make sure that everyone gets a chance to say a few words about their divorce experience.

**VII.** Administer the informal self-esteem scale *(Who I Am)* provided at the end of this session. Explain that the results will be shared at the next session. Hand out the scale and review the instructions with the students. Allow about 10 minutes to complete the scale.

*Scoring the Self-Esteem Scale*

Be sure to score the scales before the next session. Items rated as "less than others" are scored as zero, "average" responses are scored as one, and "more than others" are scored as two for all items except numbers 2, 13, 51, and 52 which are scored in the opposite direction. Although there is no absolute score to distinguish those with high self-esteem from those with low self-esteem, individuals with scores of less than 40 most likely do not have a high opinion of themselves. It may be useful to review the actual item responses of individuals with low scores. Look for a pattern. Are all of the low-scored items related (for example, all of the items on the school scale) or is the poor self-concept more pervasive (that is, a broad array of areas are scored low)? Use this information to focus the topic of discussion during the following session.

The information returned to the students should be a general rating of self-esteem (low = < 40; average = 40 - 74; high = > 75) and the identification of a specific area of low self-esteem if one was apparent from the responses to the scale (for example, poor opinion of romantic abilities, and so forth).

VIII. Session Evaluation Forms

It is important to complete the evaluation forms at the end of every session. This evaluation will help you prepare for the next session by

1. identifying the strengths and weaknesses of the current week's group performance,

2. reminding you of problems you encountered, thus giving yourself time to problem solve,

3. identifying the strong individuals in the group, and

4. identifying those students who are having problems.

Use of these forms will also remind you if you have met your goals for the session. This will help you make decisions about where in the curriculum to begin and how to initiate the next group meeting. The forms will help you decide if your strategies are working or if you need to modify your approach.

Completion of these group evaluation forms will help the group leader decide what changes may be of use for the next group of students that participate in this program. They will help the group leader identify where their groups have difficulty and also where more flexibility should be built in.

Finally, compiled across several groups, these forms could serve as training guides for new group leaders.

Name _____ Date _____

## WHO I AM   R3-1

Answer the following questions as to how you feel you compare to other kids your age. This is *not* a test. Don't answer questions as to how you think you ought to or want to be. Just describe yourself through this simple comparison.

| | Less Than Others | About Average | More Than Others |
|---|---|---|---|
| *1.* I like my appearance. | _____ | _____ | _____ |
| *2.* I talk back to my parents. | _____ | _____ | _____ |
| *3.* I like to go to the movies. | _____ | _____ | _____ |
| *4.* I like to go to sporting events. | _____ | _____ | _____ |
| *5.* I like school. | _____ | _____ | _____ |
| *6.* I participate in school activities. | _____ | _____ | _____ |
| *7.* I am good at sports. | _____ | _____ | _____ |
| *8.* I am a good student. | _____ | _____ | _____ |
| *9.* I have many friends. | _____ | _____ | _____ |
| *10.* I can make friends easily. | _____ | _____ | _____ |
| *11.* I know I am smart. | _____ | _____ | _____ |
| *12.* I am comfortable with the opposite sex. | _____ | _____ | _____ |

Describe yourself by answering the following questions as to how you feel you compare to other kids your age.

| | Less Than Average | About Average | More Than Average |
|---|---|---|---|
| 13. I am sad. | _____ | _____ | _____ |
| 14. I am honest with my friends. | _____ | _____ | _____ |
| 15. I get along well with my friends. | _____ | _____ | _____ |
| 16. I talk on the phone. | _____ | _____ | _____ |
| 17. I discuss things with my parents honestly. | _____ | _____ | _____ |
| 18. I get silly. | _____ | _____ | _____ |
| 19. I have a good time when I engage in activities. | _____ | _____ | _____ |
| 20. I feel the opposite sex likes me. | _____ | _____ | _____ |
| 21. I like to work (outside of school). | _____ | _____ | _____ |
| 22. I am good at my work. | _____ | _____ | _____ |
| 23. I like the way my life is going. | _____ | _____ | _____ |
| 24. I like the parent(s) who I live with. | _____ | _____ | _____ |
| 25. I like the parent(s) who I don't live with. | _____ | _____ | _____ |
| 26. I find it easy to be involved romantically. | _____ | _____ | _____ |
| 27. I like the way I'm handling my life. | _____ | _____ | _____ |

Describe yourself by answering the following questions as to how you feel you compare to other kids your age.

| | Less Than Average | About Average | More Than Average |
|---|---|---|---|
| **28.** I like being close to other people. | _____ | _____ | _____ |
| **29.** I like to be involved romantically. | _____ | _____ | _____ |
| **30.** I am happy with myself. | _____ | _____ | _____ |
| **31.** I am popular. | _____ | _____ | _____ |
| **32.** I trust teachers. | _____ | _____ | _____ |
| **33.** I trust my friends. | _____ | _____ | _____ |
| **34.** I trust my parents. | _____ | _____ | _____ |
| **35.** I am good at board games. | _____ | _____ | _____ |
| **36.** I am good at solving puzzles. | _____ | _____ | _____ |
| **37.** I like to dance. | _____ | _____ | _____ |
| **38.** I am a good listener. | _____ | _____ | _____ |
| **39.** I am a good speaker. | _____ | _____ | _____ |
| **40.** I like to have long conversations with friends. | _____ | _____ | _____ |
| **41.** I am fun on a date. | _____ | _____ | _____ |
| **42.** I am fun just to be around. | _____ | _____ | _____ |
| **43.** My parent(s) like(s) me. | _____ | _____ | _____ |
| **44.** My natural parent(s) are interested in my life. | _____ | _____ | _____ |
| **45.** I am a good dancer. | _____ | _____ | _____ |

Describe yourself by answering the following questions as to how you feel you compare to other kids your age.

|  | Less Than Average | About Average | More Than Average |
|---|---|---|---|
| **46.** My parents talk to me. | _____ | _____ | _____ |
| **47.** My teachers like me. | _____ | _____ | _____ |
| **48.** Most of my teachers know who I am. | _____ | _____ | _____ |
| **49.** Most kids like me. | _____ | _____ | _____ |
| **50.** I am asked to participate in activities. | _____ | _____ | _____ |
| **51.** I get invited to parties. | _____ | _____ | _____ |
| **52.** I initiate (start) activities. | _____ | _____ | _____ |
| **53.** I am a leader. | _____ | _____ | _____ |
| **54.** I can be a good follower. | _____ | _____ | _____ |
| **55.** I am a good team player. | _____ | _____ | _____ |
| **56.** I am a loner. | _____ | _____ | _____ |
| **57.** I am interested in school politics. | _____ | _____ | _____ |
| **58.** I am interested in world events. | _____ | _____ | _____ |
| **59.** I am interested in environmental issues. | _____ | _____ | _____ |
| **60.** On the whole, I feel my life is good. | _____ | _____ | _____ |

# EVALUATION FORM—SESSION ONE   R3-2

Goal Attainment:

How successful were you at explaining the group purpose and how the group will function?

_____
_____
_____
_____
_____
_____
_____

How receptive were the group members to the introduction process?   _____

_____
_____
_____
_____
_____
_____
_____

How cooperative were the group members in completing the self-competency scale?   _____

_____
_____
_____
_____
_____
_____

© 1993 by The Center for Applied Research in Education

# EVALUATION FORM—SESSION ONE R3-2 (cont'd)

Group Participation:

Identify those students who were most active in the group process. _____

_____

_____

_____

_____

Identify those students who were the least active in the group process. _____

_____

_____

_____

Which strategy was the most effective in facilitating group interaction and participation? ____

_____

_____

_____

_____

Which strategy was the least effective? _____

_____

_____

_____

_____

# EVALUATION FORM—SESSION ONE   R3-2 (cont'd)

What things could you have done to improve the session? _____

_____

_____

_____

_____

_____


Will you change anything as you prepare for your next group session? _____

_____

_____

_____

_____

_____


Specifically, how will you start your next group session? _____

_____

_____

_____

_____

_____

# ☐ SESSION TWO:  Self-Esteem

## Goal:

*1.* To discuss self-esteem and how divorce affects it.

## Strategy:

*1.* Introduce and define the concepts of self-competency and self-esteem. Through lecture and discussion, students will learn how self-competency can affect their opinion of themselves.

*2.* Ask students to identify three things that they like about themselves or three tasks that they feel they do well as part of a discussion that emphasizes how their experiences with perceived success or failure can affect their self-esteem.

*3.* To demonstrate how the environment can affect self-competency and self-esteem, ask students to share an incident in which their parents said or did something that made them feel bad about themselves as well as an incident that made them feel good about themselves.

*4.* To provide students with information about their own self-concept, discuss with the group the results of the informal self-esteem scale administered during the previous session.

## Rationale:

Self-esteem refers to one's evaluation of oneself or the degree of satisfaction one has with oneself. Some researchers have described the self-evaluative process associated with self-esteem as being hierarchical in nature. Harter (1982) suggested that children and adolescents make discrete evaluative judgments about their competence in various domains. That is, does the child see himself/herself as being good at a particular task or able to deal successfully with certain situations? For example, *cognitive competence* represents the child's perception of his/her own academic performance, while *social competence* represents the child's perception of his/her success with peers. The child also makes a higher order evaluation of his or her global self-worth. Harter maintains that the global self-worth, that is, self-esteem, is not merely a summation of the various domains of self-competence. Rather, Harter identified perceived competency in domains that the child rates important as being likely predictors of self-esteem. For example, a child may perceive competence in peer relations as desirable. If peer relations are disrupted, as is often the case in divorced families, the child's perceived competence in this area may decline and reduce the child's global sense of self-worth.

As the child grows older, successful mastery of developmental tasks also becomes important to the development of positive self-esteem. During normal adolescent development, numerous personal and social changes occur. The individual progresses toward adult stature, and secondary sex characteristics appear. Relationships with peers of both sexes become increasingly important, and the individual is exposed to a greater range of social conditions. The normal adolescent focuses on the resolution of internal conflicts (for example, control and expression of aggressive and sexual impulses), external conflicts (for example, peer and social acceptance), and a need to gain independence from the family and establish an individual identity. Failure to resolve any of these conflicts (for example, engaging in acting-out behaviors, poor peer relations, or failure to separate from the family conflict) may be perceived as incompetence, which would then result in lowered self-esteem.

An individual's self-competency and global sense of self-worth or self-esteem is based in part on the recognition and evaluation of what we do by significant others. For most children, the most significant others are parents. Parents provide a constant source of praise (or criticism) and recognition of achievements and accomplishments. Divorce disrupts this process. The parents often become immersed in their own troubles. They may be too burdened by financial and other difficulties to provide adequate support and recognition of children's accomplishments. Researchers have demonstrated a positive relationship between the child's perception of family cohesion and the development of the child's self-concept. Group membership increases the individual's sense of competency and control through successful peer interaction and increases the individual's global self-worth through the positive regard of group members. Positive regard, then, from peer group interaction may help to provide some of the support disrupted with the family disolution.

This session, through discussion, demonstrative activities, and interpretation of the self-competency scale, will explore how family structure can affect one's self-competency and self-esteem. It is hoped that positive group interactions should not only provide support but should also help in developing conversational skills that will increase the student's perception of competency in social interactions.

## STEPS:

*Important Note:*

*Every* session should begin with a few minutes of personal discussion. For example, ask what each member did during the past weekend. If there was a holiday, ask what they did, who they spent their time with, and so on. If, during the previous session, an individual discussed what appeared to be an impending or ongoing crisis (such as going to court for a custody battle), check in with that individual. This conveys the message that each group member is valued. Sharing personal information also facilitates group cohesion.

I.  In order to further promote group participation and group interaction, begin this session by drawing a distinction between the classroom and the group.

Point out the following:

A.  It is not necessary to get permission to talk in group (members don't need to raise their hands).

B.  Participants may suggest their own discussion topics. If something important occurs between sessions, sharing the event with the group could be helpful.

C.  Participants should talk to each other. It is not necessary to use the group leader as a conversational mediator. (The leader should direct comments made to him/her to other students whenever possible).

II.  Introduce the concepts of self-competency and self-esteem.

A. Begin by defining terms. *Ask the group to define self-concept.* (Allow some discussion.)

### Sample minilecture on self-competency:

Self-concept is the picture that you have of yourself. It may be an accurate picture or it may be a distorted picture. This picture is a collection of how you rate yourself in different areas that are important to you. That is, how *competent* you feel you are in certain things. For example, how well you feel you handle things like school or dating. Your estimate of your self-competency may be accurate or distorted. That is, you may feel like a total failure in school when you are actually a B student. Your self-competency determines your self-concept which in turn defines your *self-esteem.*

*Ask the group what self-esteem is.*

Self-esteem is how much you like yourself. So, the way you rate yourself in different areas creates a picture of yourself. You may or may not like that picture. If you don't like it, we say you have poor self-esteem. If you like it, we say you have high self-esteem.

B. Explain how self-competency and one's self-concept are shaped.

## Minilecture—magician analogy:

Imagine that you're a famous magician, perhaps David Copperfield. You can do tricks such as making an elephant disappear. When the audience sees the elephant disappear, they're impressed—it's magic! When you first learned to do the trick, you felt good about it because it took a lot of effort to perfect. When you were successsful, everyone congratulated you. Now imagine that you've been doing this trick for a year as part of your stage show. You do it every night, it always works, and it's not hard for you to do anymore. You don't see it as being special. But the audience, by their applause, still lets you know that they think it's special. You feel good about the show. Now imagine that you've been doing the same trick for five years. It's definitely not hard for you to do, there's practically nothing to it. In fact, you're bored with it. So is the audience. They've seen it so often, they're not impressed anymore either. They reward you with half-hearted applause. You aren't happy with the show anymore.

As we become competent or good at something, we see what we do as being less and less valued. Think about when you were little and were learning to ride a bike or to roller skate. You probably kept saying things like "Look what I'm doing mommy!" Others help us to recognize the worth of what we do through recognition of our efforts and by praising our successes. Now that you can ride a bike, you don't think it's a big deal anymore and probably don't ask your mom to watch you when you ride it. You probably do things around the house that seldom get any recognition, but when someone does recognize your efforts ("Thanks for cleaning up the living room, Susan") it makes you feel good, and competent in your ability to do whatever it is you did. Criticism, or just plain being ignored, can lower your sense of self-competency and later, your self-concept ("I failed at this task. In fact, I can't do anything right").

*Ask the students who they think has been the greatest influence in their lives.* (Many students will say their parents have been the greatest influence.) After some discussion, continue the minilecture.

The strongest influence on self-competency and self-esteem comes from the home and from your parents. When parents divorce, the immediate support system is cut in half because one parent is not there. In addition, the parent you're living with may be preoccupied with financial matters or their own problems so that they are not giving you the support and recognition you need. Or, due to the stress that they are feeling, they may be overly critical. For these reasons, individuals from divorced families tend to have lower self-esteem than individuals from intact families.

C. Demonstrate how parental comments and criticisms can affect self-esteem.

1. *Ask students to think of something a parent said that made them not like themselves.*

*Ask each member to share it with the group.*

Encourage discussion by asking such questions as:

▲  Why did that (situation) make you feel bad?
▲  How can you deal with those types of feelings?
▲  What do you say to yourself to help?

Point out that you *can* help yourself. For example, when criticized, you can remind yourself that your parents' standards are not necessarily the same as your own.

You can also look to friends for support and recognition; go beyond the family.

2. *Ask group members to identify one thing that their parents said that made them feel good about themselves and ask them to share it with the group.*

Discussion probes may include the following:

▲  Why did (a particular situation) make you feel good?
▲  How did it make you feel about yourself?
▲  Did it make you feel successful?

III. THE KEY TO FEELING GOOD ABOUT YOURSELF:

Tell the students that they need to recognize their own strengths and *highlight* those strengths for themselves. Tell them it's good to be their own friend and confide in others.

A.  As a first step in building self-esteem, *ask students to write down three things they like about themselves and share these with the group.* Be sure to ask questions that show you are interested in what is being said. Point out that we need to remind ourselves about these qualities. We each have talents that are unique to ourselves. We should be proud of those talents.

IV. Return the results of the self-esteem scale administered during the previous session. Discuss the results of the scale and point out individual areas of strengths and weaknesses. Explain that even though a person may think that they have a good self-opinion, it is often the case that there are areas in which we do not feel good about ourselves. *Ask the group how they think their parental divorce experience may have influenced their self-competency ratings.* Then ask them to generate ideas about how they can change their opinions of themselves. Close the session with a reminder to focus on strengths.

# EVALUATION FORM—SESSION TWO   R3-3

Goal Attainment:

How successful were you at discussing self-esteem and the effects of divorce on self-esteem?

_____

_____

_____

_____

_____

_____

How receptive were the group members?   _____

_____

_____

_____

_____

_____

_____

Did you alter the treatment program guide for this session? If yes, how? Was it effective?   __

_____

_____

_____

_____

_____

_____

_____

# EVALUATION FORM—SESSION TWO   R3-3 (cont'd)

Group Participation:

Identify those students who were most active in the group process. _____

_____

_____

_____

_____

Identify those students who were least active in the group process. _____

_____

_____

_____

_____

Which strategy was the most effective in facilitating group interaction and participation? ____

_____

_____

_____

_____

Which strategy was the least effective? _____

_____

_____

_____

_____

# EVALUATION FORM—SESSION TWO   R3-3 (cont'd)

What things could you have done to improve the session? _____

_____

_____

_____

_____

_____


Will you change anything as you prepare for your next group session? _____

_____

_____

_____

_____

_____

_____


Specifically, how will you start your next group session? _____

_____

_____

_____

_____

_____

## ☐ SESSION THREE: Trust, Feelings, and Sharing One's Self and One's Feelings

### Goals:

1. To discuss trust and how divorce may affect a sense of trust in others.

2. To identify the emotions that are commonly associated with divorce and to discuss what happens to feelings that are *repressed.*

### Strategy:

1. Begin with a discussion of trust; what it is and how it is developed. (Refer to the group rules discussed in Session One.)

2. Show students how their sense of self-concept will also affect trust. That is, sometimes we don't trust ourselves to be trustworthy or responsible in relationships, so we may stay away from intimate involvement with others. In addition, if we don't trust ourselves, we may expect others to be untrustworthy.

3. Discuss with the group how divorce can affect trust. The discussion will help students identify how their divorce experience has affected their sense of trust in friends and relationships.

4. By emphasizing the positive aspects of good friendships through discussion, encourage students to trust both themselves and others, and to work toward establishing close personal relationships.

5. Have group members share some of their feelings associated with divorce and how they express (or fail to express) those feelings. Sharing these feelings helps to normalize the experience.

6. Through discussion, the group will learn about what happens to feelings that are repressed and will learn to identify some of those feelings.

7. Ask the group to suggest ways of dealing with conflicts in preparation for the following sessions that will focus on problem solving, conflict resolution, and communication of feelings.

### Rationale:

Both lack of trust and repressed emotions can have a significant impact on interpersonal relationships. Learning about how these two elements affect one's life and learning to identify them in oneself not only facilitates group participation and cohesion, but will have a long-range effect on improving interpersonal relationships. Adolescents from divorced families often find it difficult to build trusting relationships due to fear of abandonment. They have witnessed the dissolution of what most individuals consider to be lasting bonds—the bonds of the family. The fear of abandonment and the resulting emotional hurt can cause the individual to withdraw from intimate contact. Yet, it is with intimate friends that individuals are most likely to discuss their feelings. Without this kind of relationship, feelings may be repressed and cause difficulties at a later date as the repressed feelings fight their way to the surface. For example, Sorosky (1977) has suggested that accusations made by one parent concerning the sexual inadequacies or infidelities of the other parent may confuse the normal adolescent's perception of his or her emerging sexuality. Accusations about that parent may cause the adolescent to feel that he/she will also be a failure as a sexual partner or that he/she will also engage in sexual infidelities. Such fears may lead to sexual acting-out behaviors. These divorce-related problems present during adolescence may persist into the individual's adult life. Typical college-aged experiences such as marriage consideration may reawaken unresolved conflicts associated with earlier divorce experiences. Such conflicts may cause the students to become preoccupied with concerns about whether or not they will be able to make their own marriages work. Individuals from divorced families are twice as likely to have seen a mental health professional, have more emotional problems, and have a higher divorce rate than those individuals from intact families.

By definition, the individual is unaware of buried feelings. Through discussion, the individual will learn to identify those feelings. Once the repressed feelings come into conscious awareness, the individual can then resolve the conflicts surrounding those feelings. In some instances, the conflict surrounding a particular feeling stems from guilt. That is, the individual feels that he/she should not feel whatever the emotion is that he/she is experiencing, so it is buried. Sharing these feelings helps to normalize the experience and hence reduces the inner conflict.

## Steps:

I. Start the session with a discussion of trust.

Begin by reviewing last week's discussion of how other people's comments and criticisms affect one's self-image and self-evaluation. Have the group members write down three positive characteristics of an ideal friend. Allow a few minutes for completion of the task. Now, ask the members to write down three characteristics that would make a poor friend. (Adolescents are sometimes resistant to written exercises. It may be helpful to have the students work in pairs and share their ideas. Ideally, students should work with someone they do not know very well, as this facilitates the development of new interpersonal relationships. This is not a critical point, however.) When all pairs have completed the task, ask the students to share their responses with the group. As they do so, create a cumulative list of their ideas. In most instances, the most common positive attribute will be trust (expressed in various specific forms—for example, being able to tell a friend anything and know that you won't be betrayed) and the most common negative attribute will be a form of betrayal. If the group has not applied the label of trust, apply it yourself.

*Ask the group how trust is developed.* From the discussion, the notion that "experience with people leads to trust" should emerge. Underscore this notion.

### Sample minilecture:

Trusting someone is a risky business. You're risking rejection. That means you might be hurt by that person. You're vulnerable and insecure. But, as we've just seen, friendships are based on trust. Trusting relationships are warm and secure and provide a basis for love. As individuals, you have seen the most significant trust relationship of life, marriage—fail.

*Ask: How did your parent's divorce affect your trust of others?* (Many students will say that they find it difficult to trust others, particularly the opposite sex.) Some people feel that experiencing their parents' divorce has made them more understanding of people and hence they feel they are better at building trusting relationships. Others wonder if they will have the same kinds of relationship difficulties that their parents had so they are less likely to trust other people. Although many marriages fail, many do not. (Underscore the positive aspects of sharing a life with someone by giving examples of the positive life events that married couples may encounter.) Some individuals feel that they will fail in relationships because their parents failed. You are unique individuals and the failure of your parents' marriage does not reflect on your value in any way. Nor does it affect your ability to build meaningful, lasting relationships. We will discuss the elements of building strong, lasting relationships in the next sections. Trust grows a little at a time—slowly. There are worthwhile relationships built through understanding, patience, and self-confidence.

II. Shift the focus of the session to a discussion of feelings.

### Sample introduction (minilecture):

During the first session, when we talked about our divorce experiences, we touched on a lot of different feelings. For the rest of this session, let's focus on those feelings, how they're expressed, and what happens to feelings that are not expressed. Think back to when you first found out that your parents were divorcing. *Ask how they felt.*

(As the discussion progresses, point out the differing emotions that are expressed (surprise, anger, fear, hurt, and so forth). If you can recall any of the details of anyone's divorce experience, ask specific questions ("Mary, you said that your Dad was having an affair with the neighbor; how did you feel when you found out?").

It is important at this time to have the students focus on the emotion attached to the divorce and to allow them time to realize that others have experienced similar feelings. For those students whose parents have been divorced for some time, *ask how they feel now. Ask about feelings connected with holidays and visitation. Ask about feelings associated with stepfamilies.*

### Sample minilecture—*feelings:*

A wide variety of emotions is associated with divorce. Each person is unique and will respond to divorce in a personal way. How you view the divorce situation is dependent in part on the circumstances surrounding the divorce (for example, whether there was family violence), and also dependent on your age at the time of the divorce. As we grow up, we have different ways of viewing the world. For example, young children, about 3–6 years of age, see themselves as being the center of the universe. Children at this age tend to believe that they are the *cause* of everything that happens around them, including the divorce. They may believe, for example, that daddy went away because they were very bad and daddy was mad at them. As one gets older, the brain begins to understand that this is not true. But the little child that remains inside all of us, even when we grow up, may still believe that the divorce was his or her own fault. Each developmental age has a certain set of beliefs about the world and one interprets life's events from that point of view. So how you experienced the divorce both at the time that it happened and how you understand it currently is determined in part by your age at the time of the divorce. Your stage of development interacted with the particular circumstances and events that led up to the divorce, leaving you with your current view of the situation.

But as we have seen from our previous discussion, there are themes that are common to many individuals who have experienced divorce:

▲ First, divorce is frightening. Some individuals may fear abandonment—if one parent leaves, maybe the other one will too—and this can lead to fear of developing close relationships. Others may worry about who will take care of them, buy their clothes, or pay for college.

▲ Some people mentioned feelings of sadness and loss as a second common theme. In the early stages of divorce, unhappiness or depression and sadness are common. When you are depressed you may lose your appetite or not be able to sleep. Some people may want to sleep all the time or eat constantly. It may be difficult to concentrate, in school especially.

▲ A third thing that can happen is that you may feel like you have to take care of one or both of your parents, rather than the other way around. Depression is common among both men and women who divorce. Some people see their parents' unhappiness and try to make them feel better by becoming the caretaker for the parent.

▲ Many people identified the feeling of loneliness as a fourth theme. When one parent leaves, the remaining parent may begin working or may start working overtime to make up for the lost income, leaving the child or children in an empty house. Plus, the parent may be preoccupied or confused and may not provide the support and attention that the child needs. Sometimes, the child may feel like he/she has to choose sides when his/her parents fight. That is, parents may compete for their childrens' attention and affection and try to undermine the other parent. If he or she feels that he/she must choose between parents, it makes the child feel very alone because the child feels he or she cannot talk to his/her parents and ask for advice.

▲ Almost everyone experiences anger, the fifth theme, in one form or another. Younger children are more likely to express anger through temper tantrums or hitting, while older individuals are more direct, resorting to verbal attacks.

All these feelings and a host of others are normal responses. But sometimes these feelings can lead to difficulties. Not everyone experiences divorce-related problems, but about one-third do. Sometimes, even when a divorce occurs in early childhood, problems may develop years later. For example, as you enter your teen years, you will go through certain developmental changes. You will begin to separate from your family and become more independent, begin dating and form other close friendships. Divorce can have an effect on this. If, due to the divorce, you find yourself taking care of younger brothers and sisters or carrying other excessive responsibilities around the home, you may have trouble separating from the family. You may find it hard to trust people and fail to develop normal close relationships with people. Again, not all individuals have problems related to their parents' divorce. One of the purposes of the group is to prevent problems from developing by identifying buried conflicts and feelings and getting them out where they can be dealt with. (An ounce of prevention is worth a pound of cure.)

*Ask the students how they expressed the things they were feeling when their parents divorced.* Try to use both general ("What did you say when you were told that your parents were getting a divorce?") and specific ("Sam, did you tell your father that your feelings were hurt when he didn't show up to see you play at the state basketball game?") probes. Many students will say that they didn't say anything.

*Ask the students what happened to those feelings? Did they go away?*

## Continue with the minilecture:

Feelings are not right or wrong, they simply happen. A *feeling* is a response to events that are happening in our lives. You can't tell yourself to feel a certain way and you can't make a feeling go away. However, you can control how you express your feelings. One way in which many people try to control their feelings is by ignoring them or burying them deep inside themselves. This is called *repression*. There are many reasons for this; for example, you won't tell your dad that you were really angry when he forgot your birthday because you don't want him to get mad at you (fear of rejection). Or you might not tell your friends that you're really scared to visit your dad because he has an alcohol problem and gets violent when he's drunk, because you're afraid that your friends will not understand and may even make fun of you. Instead, you try to forget or bury these feelings. Whatever the reason, repression is a common response among individuals from a divorced family. The problem is, buried feelings *just don't stay buried.*

## Balloon analogy:

Think of a balloon that's filled with air. Now imagine trying to push that balloon down to the bottom of a swimming pool. The deeper you try to push it, the more effort and concentration it takes. Burying your feelings is like trying to submerge the balloon. It takes a lot of effort. But those feelings keep trying to come to the surface. As you bury more and more feelings, it becomes harder and harder to hold them all down. At some point, some of those buried feelings escape and come to the surface. That is, the feelings come out in other ways.

*Ask the students to generate ideas about what happens when feelings come to the surface.* Most groups will be able to generate the concept of *displacement* (how one kicks the dog or harasses one's little brother when one is really angry with a parent, for instance). Underscore this notion.

## Continue with the minilecture:

Buried feelings lead ultimately to a loss of control. For example, if you hold anger inside continually, it may leak out a little at a time (you seem like you have a chip on your shoulder) or it may come in a sudden, unexpected explosion (you blow up at your best friend for being late to lunch).

Some feelings, especially anger, when held inside may be turned against ourselves. That is, rather than kicking the dog, we kick ourselves. This can lead to low self-evaluation. We see ourselves as not being able to do anything right (we think we're incompetent) and therefore we must be useless (low self-esteem).

*Ask the group how these feelings can be expressed.* Acknowledge the suggestions that are made but don't offer any solutions or interpretations. Conclude by saying that in the following weeks the group will be discussing the communication of feelings and approaches to problem solving.

# EVALUATION FORM—SESSION THREE  R3-4

Goal Attainment:

How successful were you at facilitating a discussion on trust and how divorce affects one's sense of trust? _____

_____

_____

_____

_____

_____

How successful was the group at identifying the emotions commonly associated with divorce?

_____

_____

_____

_____

_____

_____

_____

Did you alter the treatment program guide for this session? If yes, how, and was it effective?

_____

_____

_____

_____

_____

_____

# EVALUATION FORM—SESSION THREE   R3-4 (cont'd)

Group Participation:

Identify those students who were most active in the group process. _____

_____

_____

_____

_____

Identify those students who were least active in the group process. _____

_____

_____

_____

_____

Which strategy was the most effective in facilitating group interaction and participation? ____

_____

_____

_____

_____

Which strategy was the least effective? _____

_____

_____

_____

_____

# EVALUATION FORM—SESSION THREE   R3-4 (cont'd)

What things could you have done to improve the session?  _____

_____

_____

_____

_____

_____

Will you change anything as you prepare for your next group session?  _____

_____

_____

_____

_____

_____

_____

Specifically, how will you start your next group session?  _____

_____

_____

_____

_____

_____

# ☐ SESSION FOUR:   Problem-Solving

### Goal:

*1.* To teach a six-step, problem-solving method.

### Strategy:

*1.* Introduce the topic of problems and problem solving.

*2.* Discuss with the group problems in general, and identify problems that members have encountered recently.

*3.* Through the use of discussion and a handout outlining a six-step problem-solving technique, assist the group in exploring ways of dealing with divorce-related problems.

*4.* Have group members work together in small groups to generate problem scenarios. The group as a whole will then use the six-step technique to explore ways of solving the problems.

### Rationale:

Many individuals respond to situations, particularly crisis situations, in a stereotypical manner. They do not realize that they have a choice in how they respond to or handle any given event. Because children have little or no control over the events that occur during parental divorce, they develop an external locus of control. That is, they perceive all events in their lives as being beyond their control. The present problem-solving method is intended to increase the individual's awareness of his/her own capacity to deal with problem situations and to increase the assertiveness with which one approaches problematic situations. Knowing that there is a choice imparts a sense of control of one's life and increases confidence in the self. As a continuation of the previous session, this problem-solving technique also encourages the identification of feelings and the appropriate expression of those feelings.

## Steps:

I. Begin the session by introducing the topic of problem solving.

### Sample introduction:

Everyone is faced with problems almost every day of their lives. But, individuals that are from divorced families have an additional set of problems that are unique to them. We are going to talk about a problem-solving strategy that can be used to solve a variety of problems, including the ones that are related to divorce.

*Ask the group to define what a problem is. Ask them what problems they have had within the last week or two.* Most groups will generate problems that are related to divorce, such as conflict with step-siblings, money difficulties, and custody issues. As the students make their contributions, write them down. Reiterate the problems by category (money problems, custody issues, and so forth).

II. Introduce the six-step problem solving method: (If you are going to use the handout presented at the end of the session, pass it out now.)

Begin by saying:

We can't choose the problems that we are faced with, but we can take steps to deal with the problems. There are always choices. Having a choice about how we respond to a situation is to be in control of our lives. Review the Six steps for problem-solving.

Spend a little time explaining what is meant by problems that can be viewed as either solvable or unsolvable.

### Sample minilecture:

Some problems may be dealt with through initiating action— that is, doing some physical action that will change the situation, such as fixing something that is broken or following through on a promise to do something for someone. Other problems may be dealt with through expressing one's opinion. Oftentimes people will complain about a situation to their friends but fail to share their concerns or ideas with other individuals who are involved in the problem situation directly. For example, you may go to a restaurant and receive a bowl of soup that is cold. If you do not tell the person who served the soup that it is cold, they may not be aware of the situation. There are some problems that cannot be solved either through direct action or by voicing your opinion.

If you discover a flat tire on the way to an important engagement, there is little you can do to remedy the situation. You can, however, control your response to the event. For example, you can rant and rave and kick the tire while focusing on how frustrated you are, or you can relax and accept the situation as an inconvenience and calmly do what you can to remedy the problem.

III. Ask the group to break up into groups of two or three people. (Small groups facilitate group interaction.) Each group should generate a problem scenario. Allow about 10 minutes for this.

IV. Have each group present the problem to the whole group. Using the above problem-solving approach, discuss as many of the scenarios as time permits. It is likely that the scenarios that are generated may not be fictional, but rather an actual account of a personal crisis or ongoing divorce problem such as an abusive parent or an alcoholic or drug-using parent. Problem-solving in this case not only provides the group with practice in using the six-step technique, but also allows the individual to work through his personal conflict with the help and support of group members. Take special note of what is said and, if necessary, continue the discussion at the beginning of the next session. Information gained from this session can also be incorporated into the following session's lesson.

## SIX STEPS FOR PROBLEM SOLVING   R3-5

1.  State the problem.
    Be specific. Be direct.

    | *Examples:* | My father is an alcoholic. |
    | | I'm failing my math class. |
    | | I broke up with my boyfriend/girlfriend. |

2.  Identify how you feel about it.

    | *Examples:* | I'm angry. |
    | | My feelings are hurt. |

    Your feelings can cloud the issues, particularly if you're not really clear about how you feel. Besides, remember what happens to feelings that are bottled up.

3.  Discuss the problem with a trusted friend.

    | *Someone who:* | will listen and will not judge you |
    | | will let you talk your feelings out |
    | | will give you an objective response—not just say what you want to hear |

    Remember, talking helps you organize your thoughts and may help clarify things that are confusing. Listening to someone may help you see the problem from a different point of view or allow you to see options you hadn't considered before.

4.  Decide if the problem can be solved directly.

    Some things you can control and some things you cannot.
    Therefore some problems are solvable through direct action and some must be dealt with through changing your response to the problem.

    Distinguishing between problems that are beyond one's control (not solvable) and problems within one's control (solvable) is a large part of problem solving.

5.  Remind yourself that the only person you can change is *yourself.*

    Ask yourself what *you* can do to make the situation better.

6.  Decide what action is possible.

    Physical response (Example: close the door if it's cold)
    Verbal response (Example: express your point of view)
    Inner response (Example: relaxation exercise)

© 1993 by The Center for Applied Research in Education

# EVALUATION FORM—SESSION FOUR   R3-6

Goal Attainment:

How successful were you at teaching the six-step problem-solving method?   _____

_____

_____

_____

_____

_____

How receptive were group members to the discussion of problem-solving techniques?   ____

_____

_____

_____

_____

_____

Did you alter the treatment program guide for this session? If yes, how, and was it effective?

_____

_____

_____

_____

_____

_____

# EVALUATION FORM—SESSION FOUR   R3-6 (cont'd)

Group Participation:

Identify those students who were most active in the group process.   _____

_____

_____

_____

_____

Identify those students who were least active in the group process.   _____

_____

_____

_____

_____

_____

Which strategy was the most effective in facilitating group interaction and participation?   ____

_____

_____

_____

_____

Which strategy was the least effective?   _____

_____

_____

_____

# EVALUATION FORM—SESSION FOUR   R3-6 (cont'd)

What things could you have done to improve the session?   _____

_____

_____

_____

_____

_____

Will you change anything as you prepare for your next group session?   _____

_____

_____

_____

_____

_____

Specifically, how will you start your next group session?   _____

_____

_____

_____

_____

_____

# ☐ SESSION FIVE: Personal Rights

## Goals:

*1.* To provide additional practice with problem solving.

*2.* To identify and understand one's rights as an individual.

*3.* To identify and understand one's rights as a child of divorce.

*4.* To learn ways to communicate that one's rights have been violated.

## Strategy:

*1.* Begin by having the group review the six-step problem-solving strategy presented in session four and then engage in additional problem-solving practice.

*2.* From the scenarios generated in the last session, point out examples of an individual's rights that were violated, thereby introducing the topic of individual rights.

*3.* Discuss with the group what their rights are as individuals. Allow them to discuss ways that they can protect their rights and relay why it is important for them to do so.

*4.* Discuss with the group what their rights are as children of divorce. Review the handout that outlines some of the rights that they should be aware of.

*5.* Introduce through discussion ways of communicating to others that their individual rights have been violated. An optional handout covering the topic is provided at the end of the session.

## Rationale:

Students from divorced families often feel they are powerless. Skill in problem solving may instill a sense of control over one's life, thereby improving one's overall sense of self-esteem. Understanding one's rights as an individual and standing up for the self when one's rights have been violated serves to increase the sense of control one has over one's life. Students need to know that their rights as individuals also apply to their divorce situations. Children of divorce should not be victims or pawns in the divorce process. Yet, most students will relate stories of being asked by one parent to spy on the other parent or to serve as bearers of unpleasant messages. Some students will report instances of being pressured to choose sides in parental disputes. Many students will relate instances when they felt angry or resentful over what they perceived to be unfair parental actions;

however, most will acknowledge that they did not discuss these matters with the parent. In short, many students have not learned to be effective communicators and fail to set limits for the ways in which they wish to be treated. Learning to be an effective communicator may prove to be an invaluable life-long problem-solving skill for the group members.

# Steps:

I. Begin the session with a review of the six-step problem-solving strategy presented during the previous session. Using the scenarios generated during the last session, have the group practice problem solving. Limit this to about 15 minutes, or two additional scenarios.

II. Introduce the topic of personal rights by using an example or two from the above scenarios. Point out the cases in which an individual was treated with disrespect or unfairly. Underscore that the students are individuals with personal rights even though they may be dependent on their parents.

*Ask the students what they think their rights are.* This should include such things as:

▲ being treated fairly
▲ being treated with respect
▲ being given an explanation for decisions that affect their lives
▲ being consulted in decision making
▲ having their property treated with respect

III. Review the material presented in the handout entitled "Your Rights As An Individual":

*Note:* Passing copies to the students is optional. As was discussed in Section 2, too much emphasis on handouts and other activities may slow group development. As the leader you need to assess the maturity level of the group you are leading. The more mature the group, the less dependent they will be on visual aids. All of the material presented in this session should be shared with the group. You should select the handouts that you feel will benefit the group members most. The rest of the material can be presented in discussion format.

## Minilecture:

You also have rights as an individual from a divorced family. Sometimes parents, stepparents, siblings, or stepsiblings may violate your rights without realizing that they are doing so. They violate your rights in ways that individuals from intact families may not experience.

Pass out the handout "Personal Rights For Children of Divorce" if you choose to use it. Otherwise, simply review the concepts. (We feel this is important information and recommend use of this handout for all ages and maturity levels.)

This list contains a few of the "rights." Let's review the list and see how many more we can come up with.

## Minilecture:

Once you understand your rights and can recognize when your rights have been violated, you must then let others know that you feel you have been treated unfairly. The manner in which you do this is very important, because, to a large extent, it determines how you will be responded to.

IV. Review the information on the handout, "Taking Action When Your Rights Have Been Violated." (You may choose to simply discuss the material and not use the actual handout.)

V. *Ask the group to discuss a recent instance in which they felt their rights had been violated.* Discuss how the situation could have been handled in a more positive manner.

Name _____  Date _____

# YOUR RIGHTS AS AN INDIVIDUAL    R3-7

As individuals we all have rights. That is, we can expect to be treated in certain ways and have certain privileges.

- ▲ We are all entitled to courtesy and respect from others.
- ▲ We should be able to participate in decisions that affect our lives.
- ▲ We should be able to express our thoughts and concerns to those around us.
- ▲ We should be given information that affects our lives.

As an individual you should protect your rights. You need to do two things to accomplish this:

1. You need a clearly defined idea of what your rights are.
2. You need to be an effective communicator so that you can tell others when you feel your rights are being infringed upon.

Protecting your rights:

1. lets others know that you do not like the way you are being treated.
2. lets others know that you will defend yourself if you feel the situation is unfair.
3. establishes a standard for future interactions.

When you fail to protect your rights:

1. you may lose privileges or have less control over your life.
2. you may experience anger or lowered self-esteem.
3. you increase the likelihood that you will be treated unfairly again.

Name _____ Date _____

# PERSONAL RIGHTS FOR CHILDREN OF DIVORCE   R3-8

1. You have the right to ask to see each of your parents.

2. You have the right to talk to each of your parents on the phone as often as you like.

3. You have the right to refuse to deliver unkind messages from one parent to another.

4. You have the right to request private time with your parents without their boyfriends or girlfriends (husbands or wives).

5. You have the right to spend time with a visiting parent even if it isn't in the divorce decree.

6. You have the right to see all of your grandparents even if your parents don't like them.

7. You have the right to ask people (a parent, grandparent, or stepparent) to stop talking badly about the absent parent.

8. You have the right to leave any situation in which people refuse to stop talking badly about the absent parent.

9. You have the right to buy cards or gifts for any of your relatives (aunts, uncles, grandparents, stepparents, siblings, stepsiblings).

10. You have the right to request to live with a different parent.

11. You have the right to keep things to yourself (privacy).

12. You have the right to say "Don't ask me who I love more."

13. You have the right to refuse to spy on one parent for the other parent.

14. You have the right to talk about things that may bother you with such appropriate individuals as school guidance personnel or your minister.

15. Know what constitutes physical and sexual abuse—you have the right to avoid abuse.

16. You have the right to discuss your reasons for not wanting to see a parent.

17. You have the right to request a change in the visitation schedule if it interferes with such things as school activities or a part-time job.

18. You have the right to like your stepparents and stepsiblings.

Name _____ Date _____

## WHAT YOU CAN DO WHEN YOUR RIGHTS HAVE BEEN VIOLATED    R3-9
### Good Communication Skills Are a Major Factor in Maintaining Rights

1.  State your case.

    When you feel that you have been treated unfairly, tell the person how you feel. You need to be direct in your approach and clear about your reasons. Be constructive (tell the person how you want to be treated). Use this approach only when necessary. If you do it often, you may be seen as a complainer and you'll be ignored!

    Example: Your mother never writes anything down when your friends call. Your messages consist of "Someone called while you were out." You, on the other hand, always get the name and number of people who call and leave messages for her. What can you say?

2.  Ask for additional information.

    Many times we feel slighted or taken advantage of because we can't see the "big picture." That is, unknown factors may be at work. Asking for additional information clarifies misunderstandings and may give you additional information upon which to base your own assessment of a situation. Having all relevant information can make an unpleasant situation more tolerable.

    Caution: The *way* you ask for additional information is important. "Why" questions can make people defensive and lead to arguments and anger. Use a nonthreatening approach.

    Example: Your father fails to show up for a play in which you have the lead role. He has also failed to show up on regular visiting days for the past several months. Ask him about these things.

3.  Ask a person to stop doing something that hurts your feelings or is annoying.

    Many people are unaware of the effect they are having on the people around them (like the person who absentmindedly clicks his pen during a test). They may not realize that what they said or did hurt your feelings or made you angry. Asking someone to change their behavior can, however, be threatening and they may respond in an angry or aggressive manner, so be tactful in your approach.

    Example: Your mother has begun dating someone who she seems very attached to. For the last month, they have been coming home late at night and making love in the bedroom which is right next to yours. You feel very uncomfortable listening to them. Ask her to be more considerate of your needs.

4. Learn to say "No"!

> Many individuals get taken advantage of because they feel guilty if they refuse to do something for someone. It is possible to say "no" in a polite way. Usually, offering an honest explanation (not an excuse) will suffice.

> Example: Your stepsister, whom you're trying desperately to get along with, asks you for the fifth night in a row to do the dishes for her, even though it's her week to do them. How do you tell her 'no'?

# EVALUATION FORM—SESSION FIVE   R3-10

Goal Attainment:

How successful was the group at understanding individual rights?   _____

_____

_____

_____

_____

_____

_____

How successful was the group at understanding the rights of children of divorce?   _____

_____

_____

_____

_____

_____

_____

How successful was the group at learning to communicate effectively that one's rights had been violated?   _____

_____

_____

_____

_____

_____

# EVALUATION FORM—SESSION FIVE    R3-10 (cont'd)

Did you alter the treatment program guide for this session? If yes, how and was it effective?

_____

_____

_____

_____


Group Participation:


Identify those students who were most active in the group process.    _____

_____

_____

_____

_____


Identify those students who were least active in the group process.    _____

_____

_____

_____

_____


Which strategy was the most effective in facilitating group interaction and participation?    ____

_____

_____

_____

_____

# EVALUATION FORM—SESSION FIVE   R3-10 (cont'd)

Which strategy was the least effective?  _____

_____

_____

_____

_____


What things could you have done to improve the session?  _____

_____

_____

_____

_____


Will you change anything as you prepare for your next group session?  _____

_____

_____

_____

_____


Specifically, how will you start your next group session?  _____

_____

_____

_____

_____

## ☐ SESSION SIX: Working Through Conflict

### Goals:

1. To introduce the concepts of external and internal conflict.

2. To discuss ways to work through external conflict.

### Strategy:

1. The concepts in this session build upon those introduced in the previous session. Begin the session with a brief review of the handout on communicating rights that have been violated. Approximately one-half of this session should be devoted to a discussion of personal rights.

2. A violation of one's personal rights often results in conflict. The conflict may be between people (external) or within the self (internal). Examine these two concepts.

3. To facilitate a discussion of these concepts, ask the group members to share instances of external conflict, discussing how each handled their respective situations.

4. Delineate the difference between *conflict resolution* and *argument*. Discuss ways to work through conflict with the group members.

### Rationale:

Working through conflict is one aspect of problem solving. Adolescents from divorced families may encounter certain conflicts that children from intact families do not experience. For example, rules and expectations may differ between the households of the custodial versus the noncustodial parent, which can create confusion and conflict. Similarly, attitudes, expectations, and values may differ between the natural parent and stepparent, and also creates conflict. The adolescent often feels there is nothing that can be done to improve his/her situation. Teaching conflict resolution skills may give the individual a sense of control as well as promote the idea of compromise as a means of achieving conflict resolution.

Adolescents from divorced families may experience internal conflict. For example, they may find themselves being angry with a parent for "causing" the family breakup by moving out, yet also misses the parent terribly. They may be in a situation where the custodial parent asks the child to "spy" on the noncustodial parent during visiting days, resulting in loyalty conflicts. Such inner conflicts, although based on certain environmental events, may be beyond the control of the child. The student needs to be able to recognize inner conflict as a first step to controlling it.

## Steps:

I. Review the steps covered in the last session about communicating to others that one's rights have been violated. Continue the discussion from the last session. This should take about half of the present session.

II. Introduce the concepts of external versus internal conflict.

### Sample minilecture:

Sometimes there is conflict between two people. For example, when your parent sets a curfew of 10:00 P.M. and you think it should be midnight, there is conflict, or disagreement, between yourself and your parent. Other times conflict is internal or it exists within yourself. When you feel two different things at the same time, or when you can't decide between two options, that's internal conflict. For example, you miss your Dad because he left the family, but you are angry with him because he had an affair with his secretary.

*Ask the students to generate instances of conflict with their parents. Discuss how they handled each conflict.*

The difference between conflict resolution and argument is that when you argue, no one really listens. A solution (compromise) is not reached. Resolving conflict involves clarifying the points of contention for both parties and then reaching an agreement based on the give and take of both sides.

III. Review the handout entitled "Working Through Conflict" presented at the end of the session.

IV. For the remainder of the session, have the students practice working through conflict situations. Ask the students to review the scenarios described previously and discuss how they could have handled the situations more effectively.

As an alternative to this exercise, ask the students to work in groups of two or three to generate conflict scenarios. Then as a group, discuss how to resolve the conflicts effectively.

A third alternative is to have pairs of students role play scenes that the group leader has prepared prior to the session. Role plays with some high school students can be difficult, particularly if there are extremely shy individuals in the group. By this session, the group leader should be familiar enough with the members to be able to evaluate the usefulness of incorporating role plays into group activities.

Name _____     Date _____

# WORKING THROUGH CONFLICT   R3-11

1. Discussion.

   Discussion means that all parties have an opportunity to state their concerns. The opposing views must be defined clearly, all parties involved need to understand all relevant issues.

2. Evaluation.

   Weigh both sides of the argument to decide how big the differences of opinion are.

   If the differences are small, a little compromise on the part of both parties may resolve the conflict.

3. Bargaining.

   If compromise is possible, decide what each party will do and state clearly what the terms of the agreement are.

4. Follow through.

   Once an agreement has been made, follow through on the terms of the agreement. This will make future conflicts easier to resolve.

5. Closure.

   If an agreement has been reached, keep the lines of communication open. Show your willingness to hold up your end of the bargain and monitor the progress that the other party is making toward fulfilling its part of the bargain. If the differences are very large, no compromise may be possible. Further discussion will result in argument. Closure is established by restating your position and acknowledging that you feel no agreement can be reached.

# EVALUATION FORM—SESSION SIX   R3-12

Goal Attainment:

How successful were you at teaching the concepts of external and internal (interpersonal and intrapersonal) conflict? _____

_____

_____

_____

_____

_____

How receptive were the group members to a discussion of interpersonal conflict resolution?

_____

_____

_____

_____

_____

_____

Did you alter the treatment program guide for this session? If yes, how and was it effective?

_____

_____

_____

_____

_____

_____

# EVALUATION FORM—SESSION SIX   R3-12 (cont'd)

Group Participation:

Identify those students who were most active in the group process. _____

_____

_____

_____

_____

Identify those students who were least active in the group process. _____

_____

_____

_____

Which strategy was the most effective in facilitating group interaction and participation? ____

_____

_____

_____

_____

Which strategy was the least effective? _____

_____

_____

_____

_____

# EVALUATION FORM—SESSION SIX   R3-12 (cont'd)

What things could you have done to improve the session? _____

_____

_____

_____

_____

_____

Will you change anything as you prepare for your next group session? _____

_____

_____

_____

_____

_____

Specifically, how will you start your next group session? _____

_____

_____

_____

_____

_____

## ☐ SESSION SEVEN:   Inner Conflict and Relaxation Training

### Goal:

*1.* To teach individuals to reduce anxiety that is related to inner conflict through the use of relaxation training.

### Strategy:

*1.* This session builds upon the two previous sessions. Begin the session with a brief review of external conflict resolution.

*2.* As was also mentioned in the previous session, some conflicts cannot be resolved. Lead a discussion about the possible effects of unresolved external conflicts and how these conflicts can lead to internal conflict.

*3.* Introduce the concept of relaxation training. Through the use of a teach-yourself manual and through group practice, the members will learn to reduce anxiety associated with both unresolved external conflict and with internal conflict.

### Rationale:

As discussed previously, some problems and/or conflicts cannot be resolved. For example, a student cannot reunite the family. An individual's response to divorce may produce conflicting emotions (love/hate) that cannot be resolved immediately. Unsolved problems and unresolved conflict produce stress that has been shown to be harmful both emotionally and physically. Stress may result in poor peer interactions, poor school performance due to an inability to concentrate, and lowered self-esteem. Excessive stress over extended periods of time has been shown to be a factor in serious illnesses such as hypertension, ulcers, and colitis. It can also lead to psychological disorders such as panic attacks and agoraphobia.

Progressive relaxation is a self-control procedure aimed at reducing anxiety in order to help the individual function more fully. The procedure teaches the individual to gain conscious control over muscles that tighten during fear or anger-evoking situations. Relaxing these muscles reduces the physiological response to these emotions and creates the psychological perception of a reduction in anxiety. Occasionally, some individuals report that they still feel anxious even though the muscle groups are relaxed. The use of imagery with the relaxation procedure may reduce this anxiety by interupting the compulsive thought cycle and allowing the individual to focus on more relaxing thoughts.

## Steps:

I. Review "Working Through Conflict" from the last session.

**Sample minilecture:**

The five steps toward conflict resolution that we discussed work well when the conflict is between two people who are willing to cooperate and work together toward resolution. But sometimes the differences between the two parties are too great, or perhaps the parties involved are not willing to compromise. Even when you stop arguing there is still anger and perhaps resentment within you. Or you may be confused about the way you feel and be unable to make decisions as to how to act or respond to certain situations. This is what we mean by internal conflict. That is, conflict that exists inside of a person. When you are stirred up inside it affects the way you think and act. You may not be able to resolve the existing conflicts, but you can *control* your anxiety. You can teach yourself to relax in stressful situations. When you are anxious, you are not thinking clearly. Your thoughts seem to go around in circles. Your body is tense and uncomfortable. However, we will discuss ways through which you can teach yourself to relax and reduce this stress.

II. Read through the first page of the Relaxation Instructions provided at the end of this session with the students. Be sure to explain to the students that the muscle tightening and relaxing is intended to train the individual how to relax certain muscle groups. With practice, the tightening and relaxing exercises can be eliminated. The student should learn to relax all the muscles at once in conjunction with breath exhalation.

III. Introduce the concept of imagery.

**Sample minilecture:**

Sometimes, even though your body is relaxed, your mind is not; your thoughts race and you may still feel anxious or upset. Imagining a relaxing scene can help the mind to relax.

▲ First, begin by relaxing your muscles as described in the Relaxation Instructions.

▲ Second, concentrate on your breathing. Breathe deeply, taking long, slow, regular breaths.

▲ Third, when your muscles are relaxed and your breathing is regular, imagine the most relaxing scene you can think of. For example, lying on a beach on a sunny day, listening to the waves or perhaps lying in the grass and watching the clouds. Or how about a shady hammock by a pool, with a water fountain trickling in the background. Imagine whatever is most relaxing to you.

*Ask the students to suggest relaxing scenes.* Have the students try imagining the scenes they have suggested. *Ask for feedback.* Discuss how they felt before and after the exercise. Reiterate the need for practice.

IV. Depending upon the skills of the group leader and the cohesiveness and cooperativeness of the group, a more in-depth relaxation training exercise may be conducted. After reviewing the two page Relaxation Instructional handout, the leader may wish to guide the group members through an entire relaxation session. A sample session follows the two page handout. The session takes between 30 and 40 minutes. Begin by having the students sit comfortably in their chairs and begin relaxing their muscles. The leader should begin with a calm but directive tone of voice and pace the session based upon the responses of the group members. Watch the facial muscles of the participants. As they become relaxed, the muscles of the face will become smooth and symmetrical. The breathing becomes slow, deep, and regular. As this begins to occur, the leader should slow the pace of the instructions. The leader's voice should take on a monotone quality. Be sure to allow time between each suggestion. The time interval should become longer and longer as the participants become more and more relaxed. The group leader may wish to make an audiotape and try the relaxation exercise him/herself as a means of gauging the appropriatenes of the time intervals. (An audiotape could be played for the actual group session, but this does not allow for pacing the session in response to the members' reactions.)

When the session time is almost over, begin picking up the pace a little at a time and introduce some inflection into the voice. Try not to end the session abruptly. The idea is to maintain the relaxed state that has been induced.

Name _____    Date _____

# Relaxation Instructions   R3-13

Gaining conscious control over your body can help reduce the discomfort you feel during times of stress due to physical responses such as heart palpitations, sweating palms, and quivering voices.

I.  Positioning the body.

When you are ready to do the relaxation exercises, sit in a comfortable chair. Do not lie down as falling asleep is not what is intended. Sit with both feet flat on the floor or with feet crossed at the ankles. Lace your fingers together and place them in your lap. Focus your eyes on a spot on the floor about eight feet in front of you with your head tipped slightly forward. Now close your eyes.

II. Relaxing your muscles.

In order to tell your muscles to relax, you must know the difference between what it feels like when your muscles are tight, and how they feel when relaxed. Begin tightening and relaxing various groups of muscles. Start at the head by tightening and relaxing the facial muscles (frown). Do this several times. Now do the same thing with the muscles of the neck, then the shoulders and arms. Tighten the stomach muscles and buttocks. Last, tighten and relax the muscles of the thigh and calf.

III. Breathing.

Breathe in as you tighten muscles. Breathe out as you relax the muscles. Imagine yourself becoming more and more relaxed every time you exhale.

With practice, you will be able to relax your entire body by inhaling deeply and relaxing as you slowly exhale breath. It will not be necessary to tighten and relax all the muscle groups.

IV. Imagining.

When your body is comfortable and relaxed, try to imagine the most relaxing scene you can think of. Put yourself in the picture, and feel each sensation. Let go of tension.

Relaxation for self-control is not only helpful for divorce-related problems. Relaxation can also be used when you are angry at a friend, are in a stressful situation such as giving a speech, or are faced with other types of job or school-related stressors such as test anxiety. In short, it can and should be used anywhere, at anytime.

130

# Sample Dialogue for an Extended Relaxation Training Session

As a group, we're going to try the relaxation procedure we discussed. You will be able to do this exercise at home whenever you wish. If you take this exercise and practice it 20 minutes a day, over a short period of time you will begin to train your body to relax and reduce tension whenever you wish. The exercises themselves will naturally produce a relaxed state. The repetition of the exercises day after day will train the body to be in a relaxed state because it is the most comfortable state for the body to be in.

Place your feet flat on the floor or with your legs stretched out in front of you and crossed at the ankles. Now place your hands in your lap with the palms on the upper leg in a relaxed position. If you prefer, you may lace your fingers together and lay them comfortably in your lap. Good!

Shift your body so that you are comfortable. Please do not move from this position. With your head bent forward slightly, focus your eyes on a place somewhere around your knees or on the floor about eight feet in front of you. Now take a deep breath and hold it... now let it go. Take another deep breath... hold it... now let it go. Feel the relaxation deepen with each breath. Once more, breathe in deeply... hold it... now let it out. Good.

Squeeze your eyes closed as tightly as you can. Feel the tension that it produces behind the eyes... now relax, let go of the tension. Blink for a moment. Focus again on the spot you were looking at before. Let your eyes close again. Notice how relaxing it is now that your breathing is soft and your eyes are closed... With your eyes remaining closed, wrinkle your forehead as hard as you can in a terrible frown... hold it... feel the tension that it produces... now let go. Let the wrinkles go... let the tension go. Smooth out the forehead. Good. Take your tongue and press it firmly against the roof of your mouth... feel the tension that this produces in the mouth and throat. Now relax. Let the tongue lie comfortably in the bottom of your mouth. Clench your jaws together. Feel the muscles tighten along the sides of your face and up toward your forehead. Now let go of it. Let your jaw relax, your teeth separate, your lips slightly part... relax. Let your thoughts drift back over your face... your forehead... relaxed... your eyes and cheeks... relaxed... your tongue and jaw... relaxed. Breathe in, deeply... hold it... now exhale. Feel your face become even more relaxed. Focus your attention on your neck and shoulders. Relax the tension. In very, very small circles, rotate your head slightly, first in one direction... now in the other... feel the muscles in your neck loosening and relaxing. Good. Let that relaxation spread to your shoulders. With each breath the relaxation deepens and spreads.

Without moving your arms, tighten the muscles in your arms. Hold it. Now relax. Let them really relax now... just kind of limp and pulled into your lap by gravity. You're deeply relaxed and comfortable now. Notice that your heart has slowed down. Your breathing is shallow and very relaxed. Excellent. Relax the muscles in your chest and stomach. Let that relaxation spread to your hips and thighs. Tighten the muscles in your calves... hold it... now relax. Let go of all the tension. Feel the relaxation spread deeper into your legs. Let the relaxation spread to your feet. You're deeply relaxed now... Deeply relaxed.

You will notice that your body is now much more relaxed than when we started. But we can go further. I want you now to focus all your attention on your left leg. Notice the way it feels as it rests on the floor and on the chair. You can feel the material of your clothing as it rests against your skin, especially at the knee. You can feel your foot as it rests on the floor or in your shoe. And the toes as they press together. All of your attention is focused on your left leg. How relaxed and comfortable, how sensitive and alive. Now focus all your attention on your left leg from the knee down. You can feel your calf and foot as if all of your being is just inside that part of your body. Now all of your attention is focused on the left foot. Just the foot. Good. Let your attention focus only on the big toe of your left foot. All of your focus is on your big toe. Let your attention slide to the nail of your big toe. You can't feel it. You're deeply relaxed. Very comfortable.

Your breathing is very slow, very relaxed. Imagine you're on a warm, sandy beach. See the water in your mind's eye. The waves are gently rolling in toward the shore, one after the other, endlessly like they have since the beginning of time. Feel the warmth of the sun over you. You're so relaxed now. Hear the rhythm of the waves. Feel the rhythm of your breathing. With each wave and each breath you become even more relaxed. Very deeply relaxed now. Completely comfortable.

You will be able to return to this relaxed state whenever you wish. Whenever you are stressed or anxious, you will be able to tell your body to relax, to feel as relaxed and comfortable as you do now. Look at the ocean waves again. Notice how calm and relaxed you are.

In a moment, I'm going to ask you to become more alert. You are already becoming aware of the sounds around you, of the presence of other people in the room. But as you become more alert, you notice that the feeling of relaxation stays with you. Your body is still very relaxed. I'm going to count to three, and with each number you will become more alert. On three you will open your eyes. One... two ... three... (snap fingers).

# EVALUATION FORM—SESSION SEVEN R3-15

Goal Attainment:

How successful were you at teaching relaxation training? _____

_____

_____

_____

_____

_____

How successful was the group at understanding the usefulness of relaxation training in diminishing inner conflict? _____

_____

_____

_____

_____

_____

Did you alter the treatment program guide for this session? If yes, how and was it effective?

_____

_____

_____

_____

_____

_____

# EVALUATION FORM—SESSION SEVEN    R3-15 (cont'd)

Group Participation:

Identify those students who were most active in the group process. _____

_____

_____

_____

_____

Identify those students who were least active in the group process. _____

_____

_____

_____

_____

Which strategy was the most effective in facilitating group interaction and participation? ____

_____

_____

_____

_____

Which strategy was the least effective? _____

_____

_____

_____

_____

# EVALUATION FORM—SESSION SEVEN   R3-15 (cont'd)

What things could you have done to improve the session?   _____

_____

_____

_____

_____

_____

Will you change anything as you prepare for your next group session?   _____

_____

_____

_____

_____

_____

Specifically, how will you start your next group session?   _____

_____

_____

_____

_____

_____

## ☐ SESSION EIGHT: Problems Unique to Children of Divorced Families

### Goal:

*1.* To discuss problems that adolescents face that are unique to individuals from divorced families in order to provide insight into those problems and provide an opportunity for group assisted problem solving and conflict resolution.

### Strategy:

*1.* Begin by introducing the topic "Problems that are unique to individuals from divorced families." To facilitate interactive discussion, ask the group members to share problems they face.

*2.* As the students identify specific problems, list the problems and group them into common categories. To provide practice with problem solving and conflict resolution, begin a discussion focused on a single problem category. Emphasis should be placed on employing the methods and strategies discussed previously.

### Rationale:

Individuals living in a divorced family face problems that are unique to their situation. For example, they have parents who do not live in the same house and may not even live in the same town or state. Holidays may be spent with the student's time divided between parents. Rules in one household may be different from those of the other household. The adolescent may be living in a household with a stepparent with whom they do not get along. There may be economic difficulties in the custodial home and affluence in the noncustodial home. Children may be asked to spy on the other parent or may be used as weapons against the other parent. Some children may never see the noncustodial parent and therefore have to deal with issues of abandonment. Discussion helps to normalize the experience, clarify feelings, and provide insight into problem situations.

## Steps:

I. Introduce the topic of problems that are unique to individuals from divorced families.

### Sample minilecture:

Sometimes being from a family that has experienced divorce can be more difficult than living in an intact family. Your parents don't live together anymore. You may be living in a single parent household or you may be living with a step-parent. Your parents may continue to fight even though they don't live together anymore. Today, let's talk about some of those problems. Later on, we'll focus on different ways people deal with these problems and see if we can apply some of the strategies that we talked about last time. *Ask students to identify problems that they have encountered that are related to their parents' divorce directly.*

II. Make a note of the problems that are identified. Group similar problems together into more general categories.

For example:

Problems associated with living with a single parent:

▲ Children may come home to an empty house.

▲ Older children may be responsible for younger siblings.

▲ Older children may assume a more adult role of confidant to the parent, rather than the role of child.

Problems associated with visiting and custody issues:

▲ One parent competes for the child's affection by 'bad-mouthing' the other parent.

▲ The "Disneyland Dad" phenomenon in which the noncustodial parent provides entertainment and gifts not available in the custodial home. This can be exaggerated further if the noncustodial parent is not involved in routine disciplinary decisions.

▲ When the noncustodial parent begins dating, the child's visitation time may be shared with the date or shortened due to the parent's conflict of interests.

▲ The noncustodial parent may find it difficult to interact with the children on an emotional basis due to the unfamiliarity that may result from the decreased time together.

▲ Some adolescents have noted that visitation makes it difficult to hold jobs if the noncustodial parent lives in a different town.

▲ Along similar lines, a rigid visitation schedule may interfere with the child's social activities.

Problems associated with financial matters:

▲ Nonpayment of child support

▲ Concerns about college funding, and so forth

▲ Lowered socioeconomic status

Problems associated with abandonment:

▲ About one-half of children from divorced families see the noncustodial parent once a year or less. Many report a feeling of rejection and/or lowered self-esteem as a result of infrequent parental interaction.

III. Focus the discussion on a particular problem category.

For example, ask students to relate similar experiences. Ask about how they dealt with problems. Ask about the kinds of emotions that were experienced and how those feelings were expressed. Ask if they would handle the situations differently now than they did then. Ask for group suggestions about how a particular problem could be handled.

If a problem or conflict lends itself to problem solving or conflict resolution as discussed previously, apply the steps informally. If an internal conflict surfaces, discuss it in those terms.

IV. As a problem category is exhausted, move on to another category. Repeat the process for the entire session.

# EVALUATION FORM—SESSION EIGHT   R3-16

Goal Attainment:

How successful were you at facilitating discussion about the unique problems faced by children of divorce? _____

_____

_____

_____

_____

How successful was the group at developing insight into these problems and discussing problem solving and conflict resolution strategies? _____

_____

_____

_____

_____

Did you alter the treatment program guide for this session? If yes, how and was it effective?

_____

_____

_____

_____

_____

_____

# EVALUATION FORM—SESSION EIGHT   R3-16 (cont'd)

Group Participation:

Identify those students who were most active in the group process.   _____

_____

_____

_____

_____

Identify those students who were least active in the group process.   _____

_____

_____

_____

_____

Which strategy was the most effective in facilitating group interaction and participation?   ____

_____

_____

_____

_____

Which strategy was the least effective?   _____

_____

_____

_____

_____

# EVALUATION FORM—SESSION EIGHT   R3-16 (cont'd)

What things could you have done to improve the session?   _____

_____

_____

_____

_____

_____

Will you change anything as you prepare for your next group session?   _____

_____

_____

_____

_____

Specifically, how will you start your next group session?   _____

_____

_____

_____

_____

## ☐ SESSION NINE:   Dating, Remarriage, and the Stepfamily

### Goal:

*1.* To develop coping strategies for dealing with parental dating, remarriage, and the stepfamily.

### Strategy:

*1.* Begin with a discussion of parental dating. Have group members first relate their experiences and perceptions to normalize the experience.

*2.* Summarize for them the feelings and attitudes expressed by the group to get students more in touch with their feelings and allow them the opportunity to work through conflicted feelings.

*3.* Have group members discuss why parents begin to date. This should help to clarify the parental point of view and hopefully increase the understanding of parental feelings and needs.

*4.* Stress the importance of communication between teens and parents. Let the group explore ways of expressing feelings about such uncomfortable topics as parental sexuality.

*5.* Guide the group in discussing remarriage of the noncustodial parent and the problems and feelings associated with this event. Emphasize the possible positive aspects and suggest ways of dealing with the negative aspects.

*6.* Finally, have the group discuss the remarriage of the custodial parent. This discussion will include issues of the stepparent role, relationships between stepsiblings, and so forth. The emphasis will be on normalizing the experience and increasing an awareness of the feelings and difficulties of the other parties involved.

### Rationale:

Problems associated with parental dating and remarriage are quite varied. For example, the adolescent may feel that he/she has to compete for the parent's time and attention. Such feelings may reawaken old fears of abandonment which may in turn disrupt the normal adolescent process of forming meaningful relationships outside the family. The adolescent may experience a sense of conflicted loyalty. That is, the adolescent may have positive feelings toward the date or stepparent, yet feel as though he/she is betraying the natural parent. Unresolved loyalty issues that originate during the divorce may resurface and be transferred to the stepparent. This may serve to recreate many of the predivorce familial conflicts within the new family unit.

Adolescence is a developmental period when one learns about one's own sexuality and impulses. In general, parents are viewed as asexual and are thus considered "safe" objects. It is both difficult and confusing for the adolescent to be confronted with the sexual behavior of divorced parents as they begin dating. This confusion may be compounded further with accusations made by one parent concerning the sexual inadequacies or infidelities of the other parent. Such accusations may cause the adolescent to feel that he/she will also be a failure as a sexual partner or that he/she will also engage in sexual infidelities. Such fears may lead to sexual acting out behaviors.

It is not uncommon for one parent to begin dating an individual who may be close in age to the adolescent. This presents a difficult situation for the adolescent who may question why he/she should accept this young person as an adult authority figure. In addition, the distinction between the roles of parent and child may become blurred, with the adult and child interacting as peers. This may further contribute to any sexual conflicts that the adolescent may experience. This session is intended to help the adolescent identify and cope with some of these disturbing feelings. Discussion will also provide insight into the parent's position and points of view.

# Steps:

I. Introduce the topic of parental dating.

A. *Ask the group members how many have parents who are dating or who are remarried.* It is likely that at least some of the group members will have parents who are dating or are remarried. If, however, none of the members do, proceed with the discussion along hypothetical lines in that most students will eventually face this situation.

B. *Ask those individuals to relate their experiences.* Encourage discussion by asking questions and getting others to reveal similar experiences.

C. Summarize feelings and attitudes for the group. For example, it could be noted that parental sexuality makes most people uncomfortable. *Ask the group to discuss why they think this is so.* It could also be pointed out that many individuals express concern about sharing time with their parent's date. *Ask the group to expand upon their feelings about this issue.*

D. Have the group discuss why parents begin to date. This can be done by framing the original question in terms of why the *students* are beginning to date. The group leader should point out that parents have a need for same-aged companionship and a need to be loved just as the adolescent does. As the discussion continues, the group leader should explain that dating and falling in love with someone does not alter the parent's feelings toward the child, just as when the adolescent begins dating, it does not alter the way he/she feels about the parent. Continue the discussion as long as is necessary to establish a basic understanding of the parental point of view.

E. Turn the discussion to any conflicted feelings that may have surfaced during the initial dialogue. For example, many teens, when discussing parental dating or marriage, may say they "don't mind" or they think it's "O.K.". Yet, as they discuss their specific situations, there may be evidence of role confusion or anger. Point out that being jealous of the time one spends with a parent is normal. Sharing that time with a stranger can also be difficult. Or if the parent is dating someone who is kind and shows an interest in the adolescent, it is normal to like that person, and it is not a betrayal of the other parent to express that fondness. Some individuals feel that they must reject the parent's date in order to remain faithful or protect the other parent. Emphasize the importance of expressing feelings and concerns about the parent's dating to that parent. Discuss ways in which this can be done.

II. Introduce the topic of remarriage.

*Ask the group to share their feelings on parental remarriage.* Focus the discussion on the remarriage of the noncustodial parent. Possible topics of discussion include marriage to an individual close in age to the adolescent, marriage to an individual with children who will be residing with the noncustodial parent, visitation with the noncustodial parent after remarriage, liking/disliking the new marriage partner, and feelings of anger toward the new spouse, stemming from feelings of rejection. Ask the members to think of the possible advantages of building a relationship with the new spouse.

The discussion should include the following points:

▲ The relationship can take many forms.

▲ Reiterate that beginning such a relationship is not a betrayal of the custodial parent.

▲ Building a civil relationship with the stepparent at the very least, may make it easier to communicate to both parent and stepparent the child's need for "alone time" with the natural parent.

▲ When the child and stepparent do not get along, it may force the natural parent to choose sides, resulting in anger and/or blame being directed at the child by both parent and stepparent. A positive relationship reduces stress for all involved.

▲ Allowing the stepparent to get to know the child increases the stepparent's ability to understand the needs of the child.

III. Introduce the topic of stepparents and stepfamilies.

Shift the discussion to the remarriage of the custodial parent. *Ask the group members to discuss living with stepparents or stepsiblings.* Focus on the identification and expression of feelings, problems encountered, and problem solutions. For example, many teens will again say that remarriage is "O.K.," that their parents have their own lives, and so forth. They may however, express confusion about the role of the stepparent. For example, most are adamant about not calling the stepparent "mom" or "dad" and they resent it if the stepparent tries to assume a parental role. Younger siblings may, however, not distinguish between the natural parent and the stepparent. The adolescent may resent the fact that a younger brother or sister calls the stepparent "mom" or "dad." Try to impart an understanding of the point of view of the other situation participants (stepparent, siblings, stepsiblings).

IV. If you have elected to terminate the group after ten sessions, remind the students that there is only one more session.

# EVALUATION FORM—SESSION NINE   R3-17

Goal Attainment:

How successful was the group at developing coping strategies for dealing with parental dating, remarriage, and the stepfamily? _____

_____

_____

_____

_____

Which of the three, (parental dating, remarriage, or stepfamily) was the primary focus? Why?

_____

_____

_____

_____

_____

Did you alter the treatment program guide for this session? If yes, how and was it effective?

_____

_____

_____

_____

_____

# EVALUATION FORM—SESSION NINE   R3-17 (cont'd)

Group Participation:

Identify those students who were most active in the group process.   _____

_____

_____

_____

_____

Identify those students who were least active in the group process.   _____

_____

_____

_____

_____

Which strategy was the most effective in facilitating group interaction and participation?   ____

_____

_____

_____

_____

Which strategy was the least effective?   _____

_____

_____

_____

_____

# EVALUATION FORM—SESSION NINE    R3-17 (cont'd)

What things could you have done to improve the session?    _____

_____

_____

_____

_____

_____

Will you change anything as you prepare for your next group session?    _____

_____

_____

_____

_____

_____

Specifically, how will you start your next group session?    _____

_____

_____

_____

_____

_____

## ☐ SESSION TEN: Hopes for the Future, Relationship Building, Group Termination

### Goals:

*1.* To help participants recognize hopes and fears about the future, especially in relation to building interpersonal relationships.

*2.* To discuss feelings related to group termination.

### Strategy:

*1.* Begin by asking students to share their thoughts about how they feel their parents' divorce has affected their attitudes about dating and marrriage. This discussion is intended to normalize doubts and fears and to dispel irrational logic.

*2.* Discuss interpersonal attraction and ways of building strong relationships to increase the student's interpersonal self-competency and promote an optimistic view of the future.

*3.* Allow the group to discuss feelings about termination. Have them evaluate group effectiveness.

### Rationale:

There is some evidence to suggest that individuals from divorced families are less optimistic about the future than are individuals from intact families. Many adolescents express concern about building close, trusting relationships. As adolescents progress into early adulthood, they begin thinking about long-term relationships, marriage, and raising their own families. Individuals from divorced families may have difficulty entering into long-term commitments because of the reawakening of unresolved conflicts associated with their prior parental divorce experiences. Such conflicts may cause the individuals to doubt their own ability to build lasting relationships or to trust in the commitment offered by the future spouse.

This session will allow students to express such fears and will supply counterarguments for irrational fears as well as supply information about relationship building.

## Steps:

I. *Ask students how they feel their parents' divorce has affected their attitudes about dating and marriage.* Some students will say that they find it hard to trust members of the opposite sex, are more cautious about whom they choose as friends, are insecure in relationships, or don't expect their relationships and/or marriages to last. On the other hand, however, some students feel that they have learned a great deal from their parents' mistakes, that they will not make the same mistakes, and that they are better at forming and maintaining relationships because of what they have been through. *Ask the students to discuss why they feel the ways they do.* Point out irrational logic using universalizing statements and underscore the positive elements. (A *universalizing statement* is one which takes the emphasis off of the individual by including all individuals in a group or population. For example, instead of saying "You like to have your needs met" you could say "We all like to have our needs met.")

II. Discuss the elements of building and maintaining strong interpersonal relationships.

A. *Ask the students to list the things they think are important in building and maintaining relationships.*

B. Summarize their suggestions and build them into the following list: We like people who:

1. Like us.

2. Like the things and people we like.

3. Provide rewards such as praise and moral support.

4. Are around during pleasant experiences.

5. Live close by or spend a lot of time with us.

6. Are similar to us in appearance and/or behavior.

7. Satisfy our own needs.

### Sample minilecture on relationship building:

The people we get to know are those whom we see all the time. When people are familiar, we feel more comfortable with them and are more likely to engage in conversation. Ask yourself why you like your best friend. Chances are you'll say "because he/she makes me feel good" or perhaps "because he/she listens to me and understands me." These are basic needs. When someone satisfies those needs we like that person.

Discuss the items just listed in terms of the high school environment. For example, point out that certain groups of individuals can be identified by their dress ("jocks" or "preppies" can be identified by their cleancut clothes, "burnouts" by their black attire or heavy-metal T-shirts) and the type of music they listen to (rap music, heavy metal, and the like.) They are people who are similar in appearance, like the same types of clothing styles, and listen to the same types of music.

III. *Ask the group for a few suggestions about what can harm a relationship.*

### Sample minilecture on relationship problems:

Begin with these two facts: a.) between 40 and 50 percent of all marriages currently end in divorce and b.) it is estimated that 75 percent of all married people have had or will have an extramarital affair. Some researchers believe that this dramatic rise in troubled relationships is related directly to the changing American lifestyle. That is, more women have joined the work force, which has provided more opportunity for both men and women to meet and spend time with members of the opposite sex. In fact, they may spend more time with people at work than with their spouses. In addition, people who work together dress similarly, often share common ideas, and may have common interests. If a person is having a bad day at work or difficulty with a job, it is likely that support and praise will come from someone at work. It is not uncommon for individuals who work together to go to lunch together or perhaps stop at a bar after work. There may be a company softball team or golf league. These are pleasant experiences with which a member of the opposite sex may be associated. Similarity, association, and other common interests are all things that lead to attraction. This, coupled with the reduced amount of time spent with the spouse, can lead to relationship problems.

IV. *Ask students what they think can be done to counteract these effects.* Summarize their ideas in terms of the following:

A. Communication is important in any relationship.

### Minilecture:

We like people who like us. If you like someone, tell them. Don't take for granted that they already know this. If something is bothering you, discuss it. Remember our discussion about what happens to feelings that are bottled up inside.

B. Set aside time to do things of interest together.

### Minilecture:

This should be a give and take situation. You may have many common interests but it is nice if you occasionally share something that is of interest to only one of you. (Provide an example.) This does not mean you must give up the things that are of interest only to yourself. Remember, we need to have our own needs met or we will resent the other person and see them as selfish and self-centered.

C. Acknowledge effort and special considerations. A sincere "thank you" is rewarding.

D. Share good news and pleasant experiences.

E. Try to be open-minded. Remember our discussions about conflict resolution and problem solving. Compromise is important in any relationship.

F. Be good to yourself. When you feel good, it shows in everything you do.

If it is your intention that the group will continue to meet, end the session here. If the group is to terminate, continue to Step V. We have found it useful to get feedback from the participants at this point whether the group should continue to meet or not. The information can be used to help you with the ongoing group or to plan for future groups. A participant evaluation form is included at the end of the session.

V. *Ask students how they feel about meeting for the last time. Ask them what they liked about the group, and what things they would change.* Point out that a major part of what was done in the group centered around a discussion of problems. Remind them that talking can clarify situations and feelings and bring buried feelings to the surface. Encourage them to build friendships or seek support groups that will allow them to discuss their feelings further.

VI. Conclude by praising the group members for their efforts and acknowledge how pleasant each individual made your experience as a group leader.

# LEADER EVALUATION FORM—SESSION TEN   R3-18

Goal Attainment:

How successful were you at elicitng group participants' hopes and fears about the future?   __

_____

_____

_____

_____

_____

What were those hopes and fears?   _____

_____

_____

_____

_____

_____

How receptive were the group members in discussing these hopes and fears? Why?   _____

_____

_____

_____

_____

_____

# EVALUATION FORM—SESSION TEN    R3-18 (cont'd)

Did you alter the treatment program guide for this session? If yes, how and was it effective?

_____

_____

_____

_____

Group Participation:

Identify those students who were most active in the group process. _____

_____

_____

_____

_____

Identify those students who were least active in the group process. _____

_____

_____

_____

_____

Which strategy was the most effective in facilitating group interaction and participation? ____

_____

_____

_____

_____

# EVALUATION FORM—SESSION TEN   R3-18 (cont'd)

Which strategy was the least effective? _____

_____

_____

_____

What things could you have done to improve the session? _____

_____

_____

_____

Will you change anything as you prepare for your next group session? _____

_____

_____

_____

Specifically, how will you start your next group session? _____

_____

_____

_____

What kinds of feelings were elicited regarding termination of the group? _____

_____

_____

_____

# ☐ FUTURE SESSIONS

*Goal:*

1. Each session should begin with a goal. As discussed in Section 2, you, as the leader, are responsible for keeping the group functioning within the parameters that you have established. You may introduce other topics according to the needs of your group members. In such cases, the goal would be to present information and maximize group participation in a discussion focusing on the intended topic. The goal may address such things as helping a single individual cope with personal problems, and so forth. Goals may be generated by the group members at the prior session. The goal is the navigational chart by which the captain must steer the ship. Without it, the ship may run aground.

*Strategy:*

1. Always begin each session with current events. Allow individuals to share their important life events with the group. At this stage of group development, the leader should be able to sit quietly and allow the group to start itself. Try sitting quietly and stare at a point on the floor. Let the group members break the silence.

2. Once the session is underway, monitor the topics of discussion. If group members do not check in with those individuals who raised important issues at prior sessions, point that out to the participants.

3. If you are introducing a topic, try to pick one that is relevant to the particular group that you are working with. Each group will be unique and the members will not have the same needs. You may wish to begin a general discussion that is based on something that a member discussed at the prior session. For example, "Billy, last time you mentioned that you were really attracted to your new stepsister. You said that it really created some confusion. Let's take some time this week to discuss the various kinds of feelings that we may have for our steprelations and what the implications of those feelings might be."

4. Remember, as the group moves further into the working stage, the participants should become less and less dependent on the leader for direction. As the group takes on more independence, the leader should become more focused on challenging individuals' irrational beliefs. The leader, however, should strive toward teaching the group as a whole to challenge the individual. Insight and interpretations are more meaningful when they become self-discovery that is prompted by a group of peers.

**5.** As the group reaches the termination stage, begin preparing the students. A group that has been together for one or two semesters, may need two, three, or even four sessions to terminate. The first termination session may emphasize the cognitive elements of what has been learned. The leader may review such things as problem solving and individual rights with the group. Review instances in which participants used one of the new strategies successfully. During the second session, the group should begin dealing with emotional loss. As the group leader, you should model the expression of feelings of loss and the associated sadness. This may be done by sharing a favorite memory of a session involving a particular individual, or perhaps by your fondness for the personality traits of each individual. Tell them you will miss them and why. Ask each person to share similar feelings for each group member and for the leader. This exercise may take two sessions. At the final session, ask the members to share things they liked or did not like about the group. Ask if anyone would be interested in participating in future groups. Ask each member to share something that they have learned in the group either about themselves or about interpersonal relationships. What will they take with them when they leave?

# LEADER EVALUATION FORM—TREATMENT PROGRAM   R3-19

How effective was this educational and counseling program in helping students cope more effectively with their parents' divorce?

Not Effective                                                    Very Effective

| 0 | 1 | 2 | 3 | 4 | 5 | 6 | 7 | 8 | 9 | 10 |

Why did you rate it at the level you chose?   _____

_____

_____

_____


For your students' needs, what was the best part of the program?   _____

_____

_____

_____


What was the least effective part of the program?   _____

_____

_____

_____


If you have held the program twice or more, what impact did the dysfunctional level of the group members have on the effectiveness of the program?   _____

_____

_____

_____

## LEADER EVALUATION FORM—TREATMENT PROGRAM    R3-19 (cont'd)

What sessions are consistently problematic for you? _____

_____

_____

_____


What were the results of the students' evaluation of the program? _____

_____

_____

_____


How did the students rate your supervision of the group? What would you like to do differently
next time? _____

_____

_____

_____


Did the students want to continue to meet after the initial sessions were over? _____

_____

_____

_____


Did they indeed continue to meet? _____

_____

_____

_____

## LEADER EVALUATION FORM—TREATMENT PROGRAM   R3-19 (cont'd)

Will you continue to run this program? Why or why not? _____

_____

_____

_____

_____

How much of this program was educational? _____

_____

_____

_____

_____

How much of this program employed counseling? _____

_____

_____

_____

_____

Was this a good blend? _____

Should it be different? If so, why and in what ways? _____

_____

_____

_____

_____

# STUDENT EVALUATION FORM   R3-20

Did you enjoy participating in this group? _____ Yes _____ No

Would you like the group to continue to meet? _____ Yes _____ No

What things did you find most useful about the group? _____

_____

_____

_____

What things would you like to change about the group? _____

_____

_____

_____

Did you feel that you had enough opportunities to discuss your personal

situation? _____ YES _____ NO

What would you like to discuss in future sessions if the group were to continue to meet? ____

_____

_____

_____

Do you have any suggestions for the group leader? _____

_____

_____

_____

© 1993 by The Center for Applied Research in Education

## Section 4

# Conclusions

## ☐ SESSION RESULTS

There are many possible outcomes that can result from conducting the ten-session Treatment Program presented in Section 3. After years of stressors created by their parents' divorce, it is unlikely that a 10-week program will "cure" all of an adolescent's difficulties. Poor students will not suddenly become A students, withdrawn individuals will not become social butterflies, and deep-rooted anger will not go away. These types of changes come slowly with continued hard work over time. In 10 weeks, however, the program will provide a safe haven for individuals where they can acknowledge that they have problems and where they can learn new problem-solving techniques. It has provided a setting for participants to build meaningful relationships and work through conflicts within these relationships. It has provided an opportunity to learn new ways of coping within difficult situations.

If these things were provided, the 10-week program was a success. You cannot, however, control what the participants will take away with them. You cannot change the environment that the students must continue to live in.

### Continuing the Program

For these reasons, *we recommend extending the group's duration.* The longer the group meets, the more likely it is that the participants will assimilate the new material into their own behavioral repertoires, and the more benefit they will derive from the emotional support. It has been our experience that most participants will elect to continue meeting after the ten sessions have been completed.

At the end of ten sessions, the group should be at the working stage. That is, the group should be cohesive and self-reliant. Members come to the group session ready to problem-solve and offer support to other group members. The group has become a family and all members are valued participants. They have experienced the process as extremely supportive. In addition, the educational and self-esteem building components have provided structure and a sense of well-being. For these reasons, continuing the program will be a rewarding experience for both leader and participants.

If you have completed each of the ten evaluation forms that follow each session conscientiously, you already have a good understanding of the program's effectiveness. The Treatment Evaluation Form provided at the end of Session 10 should take only a few moments to complete. It will help summarize your impression of the treatment program and, together with the individual session evaluation forms, better prepare you to conduct this program in the future or to continue meeting with the current participants.

Your experience in conducting these groups may vary dramatically. The outcome will be affected by a myriad of factors: How dysfunctional the members of your group were; the number of participants who attended regularly; the kind of support you received from the school administration and faculty; the quality of the communication within the group. These are just some of the factors that influenced the group's success and your sense that the program was effective. Be sure to consider these and any other relevant factors when analyzing your program evaluation data. To help you plan future sessions, we have included the following information, which focuses on the long-term effects of divorce on children and how these children cope with adulthood.

## BACKGROUND:   LONG-TERM EFFECTS OF DIVORCE

Psychologists and other mental health professionals have long emphasized the immediate effects that divorce has on children. They have attempted to educate the public to meet the needs of children of divorce in certain ways. The focus has been on the effect that parental divorce creates on the developmental process during the experience of the parent separation. Now a growing body of evidence identifies long-term effects of divorce.

Problems that first appeared during the divorce may persist, may reappear, or may appear for the first time years after the divorce separation has occurred. Problems rooted in a divorce that occurred during the child's earlier years may give rise to problems during the adolescent years. Hillard (1984), for example, reported that typical college-aged experiences such as marriage consideration may reawaken unresolved conflicts associated with earlier divorce experiences. He suggested that such conflicts may cause the student to become preoccupied with concerns about whether or not he or she will be able to make his/her own marriage work.

In addition, divorce-related problems present during adolescence may persist into the individual's adult life. Kalter (1987) reported that individuals from divorced families were twice as likely to have seen a mental health professional, had significantly higher divorce rates, more work-related problems, and more emotional difficulties than did those individuals from intact families. Such studies suggest that adolescents in the midst of the divorce crises as well as adolescents whose parents divorced during their early years should be considered at risk. This notion, together with the complexity of normal adolescent development issues suggests that adolescents are perhaps the age group most in need of treatment.

### Contributing Factors to Long-Term Effects

While apparently not all children of divorced parents experience significant problems later on, a significant portion do (estimates range from 25 to 33 percent), and researchers are only beginning to identify and understand the contributing factors. At the 5-year mark of her study, Wallerstein reinterviewed her original sample of divorced-family children. She reported that approximately one-third of the children were apparently well-adjusted and self-confident. They reportedly did well in school and had meaningful relationships with both peers and family members. Another third of the sample, however, did not fare as well. These children appeared to be moderately to severely depressed, evidenced by chronic unhappiness, poor academic functioning, delinquent behaviors such as theft, alcohol and drug abuse, and intense anger. The remaining third of the sample appeared to have resumed their developmental progress but experienced intermittent feelings of deprivation, sadness, and anger directed at one or both parents.

### The Overburdened Child

Wallerstein has also conducted a 10-year follow-up of the original divorce study sample (Wallerstein, 1985; Wallerstein & Blakeslee, 1989). She described a pattern of decreased parental involvement in child-rearing activities, with adolescent children assuming many of the responsibilities for care of themselves and others. These children may become overwhelmed by such responsibility, which may in turn interfere with their developmental progress. Wallerstein identified several such groups of children, whom she described as "overburdened."

## Children Responsible for Their Own Care

One of the identified groups consists of children who are responsible for their own care. These children, now living in single-parent households, virtually live in empty houses. They feed themselves, put themselves to bed, and are expected to get themselves to school in the morning. Children and adolescents in this situation have a high incidence of absenteeism which affects their academic performance (Guidubaldi, Cleminshaw, Perry, & Mcloughlin, 1983).

Wallerstein noted that not all of these children were alone due to the necessity of the parent work schedule. Parents who were themselves depressed or disturbed psychologically were neglecting of their children's needs as well. Other parents, angry at the departing spouse, appeared oblivious to the needs of their children.

Wallerstein suggests that children of these types of parents are often left to cope with their fears as best as they can. Some of these fears may center on being abandoned by the parent or being thrown out of the house. Other fears focus on lack of adult supervision; that there will be no one to make or enforce rules, or anyone to take over in an emergency.

## Children Responsible for a Parent

The second type of overburdened child assumes excessive responsibility for the parent. The adolescent may fulfill a wide variety of roles in support of the parent such as caretaker, protector, confidante, or even surrogate parent. For example, the child may assume the responsibility for preparing meals for the parent and monitor the family finances. Wallerstein described the case of a 15-year-old girl who stayed home from school frequently to care for her mother. Unfortunately, in our experience, this is not uncommon.

## Children in the Shadow of Their Parents' Conflicts

A third group that Wallerstein identified are those that live in the shadow of the parents' neverending conflicts. These conflicts often center on custody and visitation issues, with conflicts arising from parental inability to adjust to the divorce. Disputes that precede the divorce often remain unresolved and continue to be issues of contention.

Slater and Haber (1984) conducted a study involving 217 high school students. The study examined the effects of continued familial conflict in both divorced and intact families. They noted that of the students from divorced families, 84 percent of the divorces had occurred at least one year prior to the study and hence the effects being measured were the long-term rather than the immediate effects of the divorce. These researchers found that high conflict produced lowered self-esteem, greater anxiety, and less feeling of control.

Evidence by Runyon and Jackson (1988) has been presented that suggests that loss of a parent through conflicted divorce is more damaging to the child than loss of a parent through *death*. For example, adolescent delinquency rates have been shown to be higher in divorce disrupted homes than in homes where a parent has died. When, however, the self-esteem of adolescents from bereaved, divorced, and intact families is compared, there is no significant difference in levels of self-esteem based *solely* on group membership. Adolescent self-esteem varies as a function of the *quality* of the family environment. It is the stress and turmoil of the original family environment and not the actual loss of the parent that is important (Partridge & Kotler, 1987). Conflict that continues after the divorce, as shown in Runyon and Jackson's research, may be a significant factor in the development of adolescent personality disturbances. Adolescents in such situations experience low self-esteem, feelings of anger, grief, and depression.

Kalter (1987) reviewed studies that examined the effects of divorce on boys' internalized sense of gender identity. He noted that the lack of an ongoing and close relationship with their fathers could result in boys being more vulnerable to difficulties in developing a stable, internal sense of masculinity. For girls, Kalter noted studies that showed how parental divorce could lead to lowered self-esteem, sexual promiscuity, and difficulty in establishing meaningful dating relationships. He underscored the observation that these behaviors often did not become apparent until long after the divorce had occurred. Kalter further noted that he found no difference in global self-esteem between college women from divorced versus intact families. Differences did occur, however, in selected areas of self-esteem. More specifically, women from divorced families had a more negative image of their own gender than women from intact families. In addition, these women held a more negative view of both men and women, and were significantly less certain about their ability to maintain a lasting marriage than were those women from intact families.

For many children, new divorce-related problems may develop when one or both parents begin dating or remarry. Sorosky (1977) discussed a number of issues that may surface. It is likely that the child will make comparisons between the stepparent and the natural parent. Unresolved loyalty issues may result in hostility being transferred to the stepparent and result in the recreation of many of the predivorce intrafamilial conflicts. Children may attempt to play the stepparent against the natural parent in an attempt to gain power over the parent. These issues may emerge during adolescence even several years following the divorce separation.

## DRAWING CONCLUSIONS FROM RESEARCH

Summarizing these findings, we realize that up to one-third of all students experiencing their parents' divorce do relatively well after the initial crisis. They regain their self-esteem, academic performance and growth continue, and they continue to form and keep healthy peer relationships. The other two-thirds or majority, however, have a multitude of problems related to their parents' conflicts and divorce. These problems frequently are with these students years after the divorce process is concluded. Poor academic performance, negative peer relationships, even delinquency and criminal activity can result. All children of divorce, however, even those who are in the surviving third, are affected by the experience.

### Case Study—Dana

Dana was 5 years old when her mom and dad got divorced. Dana and her two older brothers lived with her mom. For about six months, her dad visited with the children occasionally. Shortly after that, he moved out of state. A year later, when Dana was seven and a half, her mom remarried. Dana and her stepfather, Richard, immediately established a loving relationship. Her father never visited after her mother's remarriage, and Dana lost track of him. She soon started calling Richard "dad." The new family was wonderful for everyone and Dana grew up apparently well-adjusted — surviving her parents' divorce.

Dana herself had a first marriage fail when her son and daughter were about 2 and 4, respectively. Like her mother, Dana remarried two years after her divorce. She remarried a wonderful man who accepted her children and with whom they had two children of their own. Dana encouraged, even implored, her children to call their stepfather "dad." The problem was that unlike her father, her first husband was a very active, visiting parent. As a result, he was devastated and angry to find out his children were calling another man "dad." The children were torn by their divided loyalties and Dana was confused by everyone's reaction. Dana survived her parents' divorce well. Nevertheless, its impact on her attitudes and beliefs shaped her life significantly and resulted in a particular reaction to her own divorce and remarriage that was not only inappropriate but also harmful to her own children.

## ☐ RESULTING BEHAVIORS IN ADULT CHILDREN OF DIVORCE

Divorce's long-range impact most often affects three areas: an individual's anger, dependency-trust issues in relationships, and sense of esteem.

### Anger

Anger is often the result of an individual's inability to cope with frustration effectively. Divorce creates a situation in which all family members are frustrated more easily. Children are susceptible especially. They are angry for many reasons:

▲ Their sense of family is destroyed.

▲ They can no longer see both of their parents at the same time.

▲ Two people that they love very much no longer love (perhaps don't even like) each other.

▲ Children of divorce don't spend as much time with their parents (even custodial parents) as do children of intact families.

▲ They don't get enough guidance as they attempt to become more independent.

▲ They are often left to their own devices or are overburdened with adult-like responsibilities.

▲ Their parents' divorce is often embarrassing socially.

For example, the warring parents may both attend school conferences. The children may have to explain to friends that they can't be involved in an activity because it's their dad's weekend. If mom remarries, they must explain why their mother's last name differs from their own.

This anger often begins when the tension and conflict, that ultimately leads to divorce, begins within the family (between the parents). The anger intensifies through the divorce process and often continues during postdivorce adjustment. It may be expressed overtly in acting out against parental authority. It may be expressed more covertly through other acting out behaviors (alcohol, involvement in drug use, vandalism, premature sexuality) or through depression and withdrawal (often a defense for intense anger). Most clinicians are experienced in dealing with the acting out effects of divorce. Anger, however, often lasts for years, even into adult life. More easily frustrated and especially vulnerable to the normal ebb-and-flow of adult relationships, many grown children of divorce continue to be affected by the earlier break-up of their parents' marriage. In essence, anger stops becoming a reaction to their parents' divorce. It starts becoming a part of their personality. It becomes a part of who they are and how they are defined as a person.

All of us are familiar with bitter, cynical, easy-to-anger people. We comment that life must have treated them poorly for them to be so sour. Divorce is one of those life experiences that can help to create this type of adult personality. If the divorce's aftermath is filled with ongoing parental discord and conflict, this type of adult personality is more likely. If we can help adolescents cope with their parents' divorce more effectively through programs like this, we can help minimize the long-term effects.

### Relationship Problems

Another long-term result of divorce is the young adult's inability to form healthy, trusting adult relationships. With the destruction of the family unit, the child loses the primary group upon which is placed demands for his/her basic needs and his/her psychological needs. The preadolescent may worry about such things as enough food, clothing, and other necessities for a comfortable life. The adolescent, however, may find him- or herself without healthy adult role models who would normally offer guidance, attention, and help in solving peer problems and emerging sexual problems at a time when these psychological issues are critical to development. In an atmosphere where they cannot trust their environment to meet these basic and/or psychological needs, the children can become suspicious, jaded, and callous in their relationships to others. An existence filled with broken promises and unmet needs will eventually harden a youth to the extent that as an adult he/she may find trusting relationships and intimacy difficult at best. Two results are common.

## Feelings of Separation

One possibility is that the adult child of divorce, so traumatized by the disappointment of unmet needs, closes him- or herself off from other people and is never again able to be vulnerable and/or reliant on others. Friends are superficial and transient. Love relationships lack intimacy and trust. He or she complains frequently of being misunderstood in relationships. In fact, these adult children of divorce often don't understand the subtle nuances in loving relationships: cards, flowers, quiet dinners, conversations about nothing important, doing the dishes for *her*, preparing *his* favorite meal, and other things that make the *other person* feel good. As a result, their own marriages are often distant and unsatisfying. If they last, they are convenient sanctuaries for both adults who lead independent lives. If they dissolve, it is the divorce that may become the impetus for the adult child of divorce to finally get the psychotherapy he or she needs.

## Feelings of Dependency

Another possibility is that, as adults, children of divorce will become overly dependent. They rely completely on others for their satisfaction. They can't tolerate living alone. In relationships they are overly sensitive, frequently getting their feelings hurt and becoming almost paranoid about their loved one's relationships with others. They often have difficulty with rather simple interpersonal responsibilities such as talking to service people, making reservations, arranging for babysitters, and so on. Their marriages work if their spouses need and enjoy being dominant and having complete control in the marriage. If, however, the spouse wants more mutuality and support in decision making, the marriage will not last. Unfortunately, the adult child of divorce will interpret this failed marriage as their spouse's lack of love and commitment. If only this person loved them more, the marriage would have worked, it is the other person's fault. Overly dependent adults will go through several relationships before they are likely to look to *themselves* for answers.

### Sense of Esteem

Perhaps the most intractable and permanent result of divorce is a lowered sense of self-esteem. Psychotherapy may be helpful in helping angry people or people struggling with dependency-intimacy issues. These are both identifiable and have behavioral correlates that can be recognized, addressed, and altered. Lowered self-esteem is less tangible. It is a feeling. In response to that feeling, individuals will interact with their environment in such a way as to portray themselves as less competent and less worthy than they really are. As adults, they feel unfulfilled and often unhappy, yet they are unable to point to specific things that bother them. They may complain about relationships, jobs, activities, and/or interests, but their complaints are usually transitory. Basically, they don't enjoy life and don't feel good about themselves. Often they describe feeling somehow incomplete. They suffer from low self-esteem.

It is the family that provides a child with a sense of belonging. Wanted, supported, played with and cared for, the child feels valued and hence *of* value. The family unit is more than the sum of its parts. A child can't have a mother and siblings during the week, a father on the weekend and feel the way he or she would if this family were complete. Two important changes occur to the family system when parents divorce.

## Devaluing of the Family System

First, there occurs a subtle questioning about the *real* value of the family. If the family support system was really all that the child thought it was, so special and caring, how could it disappear? With this thinkng, the value once placed on the family depreciates. Ultimately, the family as it once existed begins to feel like a myth. For some children, their parents' divorce is not quite so destructive. Perhaps because some parents have the capacity to go beyond their own pain to support their children through this period. Perhaps some parents reconstruct a sense of family by bringing a grandparent into the home as a caretaker or through getting remarried. However it is accomplished, the child again has available the support, love, and acknowledgment needed for the development of positive self-esteem. If, however, this repairative process does not take place, then the devaluing of the family system and the lowering of the child's self-esteem continues.

## Loss of Sense of Belonging

This devaluing process is compounded further by the fact that the child sees less of *both* parents following the dissolution of the marriage. The necessities of work, caring for their households individually, and leading separate and independent social lives makes the parents less available to the child. So the child first loses the sense of belonging to a family unit and then must cope with reduced parental support and attention. For some children, this process is exacerbated even more by the continuation of their parents' conflict. The children may be caught in between their parents' war. Children cannot possibly satisfy what they perceive to be the needs of their parents. Unsuccessful, their self-esteem suffers even more. Finally, as some children of divorce reach adolescence, they are thrust into such adult-like responsibilities as cooking, cleaning, car pooling, and offering child care. These activities are undertaken so that the child can help a beleaguered parent. The parent soon takes the completion of these tasks for granted and frequently does not demonstrate enough appreciation for what the adolescent has accomplished and for what the adolescent may have given up to perform such tasks. When children strive to satisfy the emotional needs of their parents, it is almost always unsuccessful. It is consequently a detriment to their self-esteem.

### The Myth of Divorce

It has been an adult myth for decades that children are better off with parents who are separated but happy than they are with parents caught in an unhappy marriage. The myth is that life after divorce is somehow automatically more happy. The reality is that life after divorce is harder and filled with more responsibilities, less time, and less financial security. Life after divorce is clearly a bumpy journey for the majority of children. Anger, unmet dependency needs, and lowered self-esteem are the inevitable consequences.

The magnitude of the divorce impact and the duration of the effects of the divorce will be determined by the child's environment. Supportive, attentive, loving parents and extended family involvement are key. Alone, however, these may not be enough.

Our educational institutions must offer the opportunity to help children cope with their changing lives. The program presented here will not only help adolescents cope with their parents' divorce, but will also heighten the awareness of educators to the problems that children of divorce face. Through this awareness and programs like ours, children of divorce can learn to cope more effectively and lead more fulfilled and enriched lives.

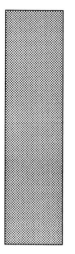

*Section 5*

# Counseling, Education, and Ancillary Programs

The ten-session program presented earlier in this resource will significantly help those students who are struggling with the devastating effects of their parents' divorce. However, with a little creative thinking, and not a lot of additional expense, several affirmative services can be added that will maximize the overall effectiveness of the counselor's efforts. The long-range benefits are significant: students will be more able and willing to learn, teachers will be less caught up in their students' emotional problems and freer to teach, and an overall atmosphere that is not only educational, but supportive and therapeutic as well will be created.

## ☐ SCHOOL FOCUS ON WHOLE DEVELOPMENT OF CHILD

For this to take place, the orientation of the school or school district must change from the traditional perception of the school as an educational institution, to school as a social service system or school as a child and adolescent developmental system. In many areas of our country, this shift has already begun. It is ironic that only when this shift is more complete will the schools be able to get back to what they were intended to do—teach academics. Drug education, sex education, and education about the adverse effects of smoking and alcohol have already become part of most curricula in school districts across the country. Many schools are now used as adult education centers in the evenings; many allow public service groups such as Alcoholics Anonymous to use their facilities; and many schools are open to the students during noneducational hours (in the evenings and on weekends) as recreational centers. The concept of the school or school system as a total developmental program for the child-adolescent and their families can be expanded easily to include an educational and therapeutic approach to the problems of children of divorce. With the ten-session group program as the cornerstone, there are adjunctive programs that can be offered that will greatly benefit the children of divorce, their families, and the rest of the community in general. One such program is in-service training for teachers and other school personnel.

## ☐ IN-SERVICE TRAINING FOR TEACHERS

With about half of the married couples in the United States getting divorced, it is imperative that teachers at all grade levels become more sensitive to the special circumstances and needs of children of divorce. In addition, many teachers are products of divorced homes or will themselves get divorced. Children of divorce are affected in numerous ways. They lose their sense of family and often simultaneously lose their homes, friends, and community. Education, which may have been a personal or family priority, now may take a backseat to survival. To understand this completely and to become more sensitive to their problems, teachers need in-service training.

Attorneys, psychologists, and even judges could be called upon to help school systems provide the necessary training. Too often schools lean toward contracting with "fee for training" courses or lecturers to provide this service. This training can be provided without cost by local groups such as the county bar association and the state psychological association. Members of these organizations have years of experience dealing with the multitide of problems created for children when their parents divorce. Working with these organizations in conjunction with some supplemental reading will educate and sensitize the teacher to the special circumstances of these children. As such, they will be far more effective.

## ☐ FEEDBACK WELCOME

As the developers of this program, we are keenly interested in your assessment of its effectiveness and want to remain available to school couselors to answer questions and give advice for additional strategies when you or another group leader feels there are problems with the current format. Also, we are constantly adding to our own experience in the field and appreciate the mutual benefit that can be gained from this additional knowledge. To this end, we would encourage you to contact us at the address listed below here. We would also encourage you to send us copies of your completed evaluation forms, either for our information or for help in solving problems you may be experiencing in conducting this educational and counseling program.

Dr. Robert Shapiro & Associates
125 S. Bloomingdale Rd.
Suite 12
Bloomingdale, Illinois 60108

# References

Bureau of the Census (1990). *Statistical Abstract of the United States 1990* (110th ed.). Washington, D.C.: U.S. Department of Commerce.

Guidubaldi, J., Cleminshaw, H.K., Perry, J.D., & Mcloughlin, C.S. (1983). The impact of parental divorce on children: Report of the nationwide NASP study. *School Psychology Review*, 12, 300-323.

Harter, S. (1982). The perceived competence scale for children. *Child Development*, 53, 87-97.

Hillard, J.R. (1984). Reactions of college students to parental divorce. *Psychiatric Annals*, 14, 663-670.

Kalter, N. (1987). Long-term effects of divorce on children: A developmental vulnerability model. *American Journal of Orthopsychiatry*, 57, 587-600.

Partridge, S., & Kotler, T. (1987). Self-esteem and adjustment in adolescents from bereaved, divorced, and intact families: Family type versus family environment. *Australian Journal of Psychology*, 39, 223-234.

Runyon, N., & Jackson, P.L. (1988). Divorce: Its impact on children. *Perspectives in Psychiatric Care*, 23, 101-105.

Slater, E.J., & Haber, J.D. (1984). Adolescent adjustment following divorce as a function of familial conflict. *Journal of Consulting and Clinical Psychology,* 52, 920-921.

Sorosky, A.D. (1977). The psychological effects of divorce on adolescents. *Adolescence*, 12, 123-136.

Wallerstein, J.S. (1985). The overburdened child: Some long-term consequences of divorce. *Social Work*, 30, 116-123.

Wallerstein, J.S., & Blakeslee, S. (1989). *Second Chances*. New York: Ticknor & Fields.

Wallerstein, J S., & Kelly, J.B. (1980). *Surviving the Breakup*. New York: Basic Books.

Yalom, I.D. (1985). *The Theory and Practice of Group Psychotherapy*. New York: Basic Books.

# Bibliography and Suggested Reading

Biller, H.B. (1981a). Father absence, divorce, and personality development. In M.E. Lamb (Ed.), *The Role of Father in Child Development* (2nd ed., pp. 489–552). New York: John Wiley.

Biller, H.B. (1981b). The father and sex role development. In M.E. Lamb (Ed.), *The Role of Father in Child Development* (2nd ed., pp. 89–156). New York: John Wiley.

Bonkowski, S.E., Bequette, S.Q., & Boomhower, S. (1982). A group design to help children adjust to parental divorce. *Social Casework: The Journal of Contemporary Social Work, 65,* 131–137.

Cantor, D.W. (1977). School-based groups for children of divorce. *Journal of Divorce,* 1, 183–187.

Carlson, C.I. (1987). Helping students deal with divorce-related issues. *Special Services in the Schools, 3,* 121–138.

Coffman, S.G., & Roark, A.E. (1988). Likely candidates for group counseling: Adolescents with divorced parents. *School Counselor,* 35, 246–252.

Cooper, J.E., Holman, J., & Braithwaite, V.A. (1983). Self–esteem and family cohesion: The child's perspective and adjustment. *Journal of Marriage and the Family,* 45, 153–159.

Drake, E.A., & Schellenberger, S. (1981). Children of separation and divorce: A review of school programs and implications for the psychologist. *School Psychology Review,* 10, 54–61.

Farber, S.S., Primavera, J., & Felner, R.D. (1984). Older adolescents and parental divorce: Adjustment problems and mediators of coping. *Journal of Divorce,* 7, 59–75.

Glenwick, D.S., & Mowrey, J.D. (1986). When parent becomes peer: Loss of intergenerational boundaries in single parent families. *Family Relations,* 35, 57–62.

Gullotta, T. (1981). Children of divorce: Easing the transition from a nuclear family. *Journal of Early Adolescence,* 1, 357–364.

Hetherington, E.M. (1972). Effects of father absence on personality development in adolescent daughters. *Developmental Psychology,* 7, 313–326.

Hetherington, E.M. (1979). Divorce: A child's perspective. *American Psychologist,* 34, 851–858.

Hetherington, E.M., Cox, M., & Cox, R. (1979). Play and social interaction in children following divorce. *Journal of Social Issues,* 35, 26–49.

Hillard, J.R. (1984). Reactions of college students to parental divorce. *Psychiatric Annals,* 14, 663–670.

Holzman, T. (1984). Schools can provide help for the children of divorce. *American School Board Journal,* 171, 46–47.

Hodges, W.F. (1986). *Interventions for Children of Divorce.* New York: John Wiley & Sons.

Kalter, N., Riemer, B., Brickman, A., & Chen, J. (1985). Implications of parental divorce for female development. *Journal of the American Academy of Child Psychiatry,* 24, 538–544.

Kalter, N., & Rubin, S. (1989, August). *Time-Limited Developmental Facilitation Groups for Children of Divorce.* Paper presented at the 97th Annual Convention of the American Psychological Association, New Orleans, LA.

Kieffer, D. (1982). Children coping with divorce: School psychological management and treatment. In J. Grimes (Ed.), *Psychological Approaches to Problems of Children and Adolescents* (pp. 89–122). Des Moines, IA: Iowa State Dept. of Public Instruction.

Kulka, R., & Weingarten, H. (1979). The long-term effects of parental divorce in childhood on adult adjustment. *Journal of Social Issues,* 35, 50–78.

Kurdek, L.A. (1981). An integrative perspective on children's divorce adjustment. *American Psychologist,* 36, 856–866.

Kurdek, L.A., & Sinclair, R.J. (1988). Adjustment of young adolescents in two-parent nuclear, stepfather, and mother-custody families. *Journal of Consulting and Clinical Psychology, 52,* 91–96.

Loers, D.L., & Prentice, D.G. (1988, August). *Children of Divorce: Group Treatment in a School Setting.* Paper presented at the 96th Annual Meeting of the American Psychological Association, Atlanta, GA.

Lowery, C.R., & Settle, S.A. (1985). Effects of divorce on children: Differential impact of custody and visitation patterns. *Family Relations, 34,* 455–463.

Luepnitz, D.A. (1979). Which aspects of divorce affect children? *Family Coordinator, 28,* 79–85.

Omizo, M.M., & Omizo, S.A. (1988). The effects of participation in group counseling sessions on self-esteem and locus of control among adolescents from divorced families. *The School Counselor, 36,* 54–60.

Pedro–Carroll, J.L., & Cowen, E.L. (1985). The children of divorce intervention program: An investigation of the efficacy of a school-based prevention program. *Journal of Consulting and Clinical Psychology, 53,* 603–611.

Saucier, J.F., & Ambert, A.M. (1982). Parental marital status and adolescents' optimism about their future. *Journal of Youth and Adolescence, 11,* 345–354.

Wallerstein, J.S. (1983). Children of divorce: The psychological tasks of the child. *American Journal of Orthopsychiatry,* 53, 230– 243.

Wallerstein, J.S. (1984). Children of divorce: Preliminary report of a ten-year follow-up of young children. *American Journal of Orthopsychiatry,* 54, 444–458.

Wallerstein, J.S., & Kelly, J.B. (1975). The effects of parental divorce: Experiences of the preschool child. *Journal of the American Academy of Child Psychiatry, 14,* 600–616.

Wallerstein, J.S., & Kelly, J.B. (1976). The effects of parental divorce experiences of the child in later latency. *American Journal of Orthopsychiatry,* 46, 256–269.

Wallerstein, J.S., & Kelly, J.B. (1979). Children and divorce: A review. *Social Work, 24,* 468–475.

Weiss, R.S. (1979). Growing up a little faster: The experience of growing up in a single-parent household. *Journal of Social Issues, 35,* 97–111.

Westman, J. (1983). The impact of divorce on teenagers. *Clinical Pediatrics, 22,* 692–697.

Wiehe, V.R. (1985). Self-esteem, attitude toward parents, and locus of control in children of divorced and nondivorced families. *Journal of Social Service Research, 8,* 17–28.

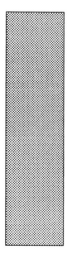

# Forms

Forms have been reproduced here *without page numbers* for easy access and copying.

- ▲ Adjustment Scale (R1-1)
- ▲ Divorce Destructiveness Scale (R1-2)
- ▲ Checklist for Forming Divorce Groups (R2-1)
- ▲ Student Identification Form (R2-2)
- ▲ Teacher Notification Form (R2-4)
- ▲ **Who I Am** Self-Esteem Scale (R3-1)
- ▲ Evaluation Forms (appropriate for any session)
- ▲ Six Steps for Problem Solving (R3-5)
- ▲ Your Rights as an Individual (R3-7)
- ▲ Personal Rights for Children of Divorce (R3-8)
- ▲ What You Can Do When Your Rights Have Been Violated (R3-9)
- ▲ Working Through Conflict (R3-11)
- ▲ Relaxation Instructions (R3-13)
- ▲ Student Evaluation Form (R3-20)

# ADJUSTMENT SCALE   R1-1

## (Instructors sheet)

Please check the appropriate column. Rate the student's level of functioning *prior* to divorce.

1.  What kind of student was the individual prior to the divorce (Was he/she attentive in class, did he/she complete assignments)?

    _____ *poor*  _____ *average*  _____ *good*

2.  How was the student's attendance?

    _____ *poor*  _____ *average*  _____ *good*

3.  What kind of grades did the student earn?

    _____ *poor*  _____ *average*  _____ *good*

4.  Did the student attend  school functions or athletic events?

    _____ *never*  _____ *seldom*  _____ *often*

5.  Did the student have any learning disabilities (such as a reading disability)?

    _____ *severe*  _____ *mild*  _____ *none*

6.  Did the student have Attention Deficit-Hyperactivity Disorder?

    _____ *severe*  _____ *slight*  _____ *none*

7.  Was the student socially accepted by the student population in general?

    _____ *no*  _____ *somewhat*  _____ *yes*

8.  Did the student have close friendships?

    _____ *no*  _____ *average amount*  _____ *yes*

9.  Was the student liked/accepted by the faculty?

    _____ *no*  _____ *somewhat*  _____ *yes*

10. Did the student spend a great deal of time alone?

    _____ *yes*  _____ *somewhat*  _____ *no*

11. Did the student have any physical handicaps?

    _____ *yes*  _____ *common ones such as glasses or braces*  _____ *none*

# ADJUSTMENT SCALE   R1-1 (continued)
## (Instructor's sheet)

12. How was the student's health?

      _poor_      _average_      _good_

13. Rate the student's verbal skills.

      _poor_      _average_      _good_

14. Was the student involved in drug or alcohol abuse?

      _yes_      _unknown_      _no_

15. Was the student's dress similar to that of his/her peers?

      _bizarre_      _average_      _fashionable_

16. Did the student engage in unusual or bizarre behavior?

      _bizarre_      _immature_      _normal_

17. Rate the student's belief system.

      _bizarre_      _immature_      _well-structured_

18. Rate the student's organizational skills.

      _poor_      _average_      _good_

19. Did the student have plans for the future?

      _no_      _vague_      _well-defined_

20. Was the student aware of, and interested in, current events?

      _no_      _somewhat_      _yes_

Name _____ Date _____

# DIVORCE DESTRUCTIVENESS SCALE   R1-2

*Please put an "X" in the appropriate column.*

|  |  | Yes | No |
|---|---|---|---|
| 1. | When your parents decided to get a divorce, did they separate between two weeks to two months after telling you about it? | _____ | _____ |
| 2. | Did your parents tell you about the divorce? | _____ | _____ |
| 3. | Did your parents avoid blaming each other for the divorce? | _____ | _____ |
| 4. | Do your parents avoid blaming each other now? | _____ | _____ |
| 5. | Did your parents avoid fighting over custody? | _____ | _____ |
| 6. | Were you asked to make a choice about which parent you wanted to live with? | _____ | _____ |
| 7. | Did you remain in the same school after the divorce? | _____ | _____ |
| 8. | Did you stay in your own home after the divorce? | _____ | _____ |
| 9. | Immediately after the divorce, did the noncustodial parent (the one you do Not live with) live within a half-hour's drive from your house? | _____ | _____ |
| 10. | Does the noncustodial parent now reside within a half-hour's drive from your house? | _____ | _____ |
| 11. | After the divorce, did you see the noncustodial parent on at least 5 days out of the month? | _____ | _____ |
| 12. | Do you now see the noncustodial parent on at least 5 days out of the month? | _____ | _____ |

# DIVORCE DESTRUCTIVENESS SCALE  R1-2 (continued)

|  | | *Yes* | *No* |
|---|---|---|---|
| 13. | Do you talk to the noncustodial parent on the phone between visits? | _____ | _____ |
| 14. | Is the parent that you live with supportive of visitation with the noncustodial parent? | _____ | _____ |
| 15. | When you are with one parent, does he/she avoid making unpleasant comments about the other parent? | _____ | _____ |
| 16. | Is the visitation schedule flexible? | _____ | _____ |
| 17. | Do your parents avoid discussing money (such as child support) in front of you or with you? | _____ | _____ |
| 18. | Does the parent with whom you live respond in a pleasant manner when you receive a gift from the noncustodial parent? | _____ | _____ |
| 19. | Does the parent you live with attend activities that you participate in (such as athletic events or school plays)? | _____ | _____ |
| 20. | Does the noncustodial parent attend such activities? | _____ | _____ |
| 21. | Do you feel that your parents get along okay since the divorce? | _____ | _____ |
| 22. | If you have brothers and/or sisters, do you all live together (or do some live with one parent and some with the other)? | _____ | _____ |
| 23. | If you live with a stepparent, do you get along with the stepparent? | _____ | _____ |
| 24. | If you live in a stepparent family, do you get along with stepbrothers and/or stepsisters? | _____ | _____ |
| 25. | Have you received any type of counseling to help you with your parents' divorce? | _____ | _____ |

# Checklist for Forming Divorce Groups   R2-1

*1.* Identify the students.

    a.  Examine school records

    b.  Solicit referrals (nurse, teachers, students, counselors)

    c.  Send parent newsletters

    d.  Visit classes to elicit self-referrals

*2.* Interview the candidates

    a.  Explain the group to the student

    b.  Complete the Student Information Form

*3.* Set up the group

    a.  Establish a size—between 6 and 10 students

    b.  Meet during the regular school day if possible

    c.  Schedule on a rotating basis so that students do not miss the same class repeatedly

    d.  Notify teachers of anticipated absences

    e.  Send reminders to students for meeting time and place

*4.* Termination

    a.  Decide if the group will meet for 10 sessions or continue beyond the defined sessions.

    b.  Explain the new parameters, should the group continue.

# STUDENT IDENTIFICATION FORM   R2-2
## (Instructor's Sheet)

Student's name: _____

Year in school: _____

Birthdate: _____   Age: _____

Number of years at this school: _____

Has student participated in prior groups at this school? _____

Has student participated in other divorce groups? _____ Where? ___

_____

Date of initial interview _____

Date of entry into group _____

Notes _____

_____

_____

_____

_____

Student's age at time of parent's seperation: _____

Student's age at time of parent's divorce: _____

Siblings:

    age: _____ sex: _____ male: _____ female: _____

    age: _____ sex: _____ male: _____ female: _____

    age: _____ sex: _____ male: _____ female: _____

With which parent does student live? _____ mother _____ father

Are all siblings living together? _____ yes _____ no

If no, with whom do they live? _____

_____

_____

# STUDENT IDENTIFICATION FORM   R2-2 (continued)
## (Instructor's Sheet)

How did the student find out about the group?

    A)   Student referral   _____

    B)   Teacher referral   _____

    C)   Counselor referral   _____

    D)   Other   _____

| | | |
|---|---|---|
| Does the student live with a stepparent? | yes | no |
| Does the student live with a stepsibling? | yes | no |
| Does the student live with half-siblings? | yes | no |
| Does the student visit the noncustodial parent? | yes | no |
| Is there a stepparent present during visitation? | yes | no |
| Are there step-siblings present during visitation? | yes | no |
| Are there half-siblings present during visitation? | yes | no |

Notes: _____

_____

_____

_____

_____

# TEACHER NOTIFICATION FORM   R2-4

Date: _____

To:

From:

The following students will be participating in a support group formed by the guidance department. The group will meet once a week, for ten weeks, for an entire class period. The scheduled time will rotate through five class periods. Students will be told that they are expected to make up any missed work whenever possible, and that they should report to the classroom on days when exams are scheduled. If you have any questions, please contact the school guidance office.

Student Name                Period to be Missed                Date

Name _____ Date _____

# WHO I AM  R3-1

Answer the following questions as to how you feel you compare to other kids your age. This is <u>not</u> a test. Don't answer questions as to how you think you ought to or want to be. Just describe yourself through this simple comparison.

|  | Less Than Others | About Average | More Than Others |
|---|---|---|---|
| 1. I like my appearance. | _____ | _____ | _____ |
| 2. I talk back to my parents. | _____ | _____ | _____ |
| 3. I like to go to the movies. | _____ | _____ | _____ |
| 4. I like to go to sporting events. | _____ | _____ | _____ |
| 5. I like school. | _____ | _____ | _____ |
| 6. I participate in school activities. | _____ | _____ | _____ |
| 7. I am good at sports. | _____ | _____ | _____ |
| 8. I am a good student. | _____ | _____ | _____ |
| 9. I have many friends. | _____ | _____ | _____ |
| 10. I can make friends easily. | _____ | _____ | _____ |
| 11. I know I am smart. | _____ | _____ | _____ |
| 12. I am comfortable with the opposite sex. | _____ | _____ | _____ |

Describe yourself by answering the following questions as to how you feel you compare to other kids your age.

| | Less Than Average | About Average | More Than Average |
|---|---|---|---|
| 13. I am sad. | _____ | _____ | _____ |
| 14. I am honest with my friends. | _____ | _____ | _____ |
| 15. I get along well with my friends. | _____ | _____ | _____ |
| 16. I talk on the phone. | _____ | _____ | _____ |
| 17. I discuss things with my parents honestly. | _____ | _____ | _____ |
| 18. I get silly. | _____ | _____ | _____ |
| 19. I have a good time when I engage in activities. | _____ | _____ | _____ |
| 20. I feel the opposite sex likes me. | _____ | _____ | _____ |
| 21. I like to work (outside of school). | _____ | _____ | _____ |
| 22. I am good at my work. | _____ | _____ | _____ |
| 23. I like the way my life is going. | _____ | _____ | _____ |
| 24. I like the parent(s) that I live with. | _____ | _____ | _____ |
| 25. I like the parent(s) that I don't live with. | _____ | _____ | _____ |
| 26. I find it easy to be involved romantically. | _____ | _____ | _____ |
| 27. I like the way I'm handling my life. | _____ | _____ | _____ |

Describe yourself by answering the following questions as to how you feel you compare to other kids your age.

|  | Less Than Average | About Average | More Than Average |
|---|---|---|---|
| 28. I like being close to other people. | _____ | _____ | _____ |
| 29. I like to be involved romantically. | _____ | _____ | _____ |
| 30. I am happy with myself. | _____ | _____ | _____ |
| 31. I am popular. | _____ | _____ | _____ |
| 32. I trust teachers. | _____ | _____ | _____ |
| 33. I trust my friends. | _____ | _____ | _____ |
| 34. I trust my parents. | _____ | _____ | _____ |
| 35. I am good at board games. | _____ | _____ | _____ |
| 36. I am good at solving puzzles. | _____ | _____ | _____ |
| 37. I like to dance. | _____ | _____ | _____ |
| 38. I am a good listener. | _____ | _____ | _____ |
| 39. I am a good speaker. | _____ | _____ | _____ |
| 40. I like to have long conversations with friends. | _____ | _____ | _____ |
| 41. I am fun on a date. | _____ | _____ | _____ |
| 42. I am fun just to be around. | _____ | _____ | _____ |
| 43. My parent(s) like(s) me. | _____ | _____ | _____ |
| 44. My natural parent(s) are interested in my life. | _____ | _____ | _____ |
| 45. I am a good dancer. | _____ | _____ | _____ |

Describe yourself by answering the following questions as to how you feel you compare to other kids your age.

|  | Less Than Average | About Average | More Than Average |
|---|---|---|---|
| 46. My parents talk to me. | _____ | _____ | _____ |
| 47. My teachers like me. | _____ | _____ | _____ |
| 48. Most of my teachers know who I am. | _____ | _____ | _____ |
| 49. Most kids like me. | _____ | _____ | _____ |
| 50. I am asked to participate in activities. | _____ | _____ | _____ |
| 51. I get invited to parties. | _____ | _____ | _____ |
| 52. I initiate (start) activities. | _____ | _____ | _____ |
| 53. I am a leader. | _____ | _____ | _____ |
| 54. I can be a good follower. | _____ | _____ | _____ |
| 55. I am a good team player. | _____ | _____ | _____ |
| 56. I am a loner. | _____ | _____ | _____ |
| 57. I am interested in school politics. | _____ | _____ | _____ |
| 58. I am interested in world events. | _____ | _____ | _____ |
| 59. I am interested in environmentali ssues. | _____ | _____ | _____ |
| 60. On the whole, I feel my life is good. | _____ | _____ | _____ |

# EVALUATION FORM

*(appropriate for any session)*

Goal Attainment:

How successful were you at explaining the group purpose and how the group will function?

_____

_____

_____

_____

_____

How receptive were the group members to the introduction process?  _____

_____

_____

_____

_____

_____

_____

How cooperative were the group members in completing the self-competency scale?  _____

_____

_____

_____

_____

_____

_____

# EVALUATION FORM   (continued)

Group Participation:

Identify those students who were most active in the group process.   _____

_____

_____

_____

_____

Identify those students who were the least active in the group process.   _____

_____

_____

_____

_____

Which strategy was the most effective in facilitating group interaction and participation?   ____

_____

_____

_____

_____

Which strategy was the least effective?   _____

_____

_____

_____

_____

# EVALUATION FORM   (continued)

What things could you have done to improve the session?   _____

_____

_____

_____

_____

_____


Will you change anything as you prepare for your next group session?   _____

_____

_____

_____

_____

_____


Specifically, how will you start your next group session?   _____

_____

_____

_____

_____

_____

# SIX STEPS FOR PROBLEM SOLVING   R3-5

1. Identify the problem.
   Be specific. Be direct.

   *Examples:*     My father is an alcoholic.
                   I'm failing my math class.
                   I broke up with my boyfriend/girlfriend.

2. Identify how you feel about it.

   *Examples:*     I'm angry.
                   My feelings are hurt.

   Your feelings can cloud the issues, particularly if you're not really clear about how you feel. Besides, remember what happens to feelings that are bottled up.

3. Discuss the problem with a trusted friend.

   *Someone who:*  will listen and will not judge you
                   will let you talk your feelings out
                   will give you an objective response - not just say what you want to hear

   Remember, talking helps you organize your thoughts and may clarify things that are confusing. Listening to someone may may help you see the problem from a different point of view or help you see options you hadn't considered before.

4. Decide if the problem can be solved directly.

   Some things you can control and some things you cannot.
   Therefore some problems are solvable through direct action and some must be dealt with through changing how you respond to the problem.

   Distinguishing between problems that are beyond one's control (not sovable) and problems within one's control (solvable) is a large part of problem solving.

5. Remind yourself that the only person you can change is *yourself.*

   Ask yourself what *you* can do to make it better.

6. Decide what action is possible.

   Physical response (Example: close the door if it's cold)
   Verbal response (Example: express your point of view)
   Inner response (Example: relaxation exercise)

Name _____     Date _____

# YOUR RIGHTS AS AN INDIVIDUAL    R3-7

As individuals we all have rights. That is, we can expect to be treated in certain ways and have certain privileges.

- ▲ We are all entitled to courtesy and respect from others.
- ▲ We should be able to participate in decisions that affect our lives.
- ▲ We should be able to express our thoughts and concerns to those around us.
- ▲ We should be given information that affects our lives.

As an individual you should protect your rights. You need to do two things to accomplish this:

1. You need a clearly defined idea of what your rights are.
2. You need to be an effective communicator so that you can tell others when you feel your rights are being infringed upon.

Protecting your rights:

1. lets others know that you do not like the way you are being treated.
2. lets others know that you will defend yourself if you feel the situation is unfair.
3. establishes a standard for future interactions.

When you fail to protect your rights:

1. you may lose privileges or have less control over your life.
2. you may experience anger or lowered self-esteem.
3. you increase the likelihood that you will be treated unfairly again.

Name _____  Date _____

# PERSONAL RIGHTS FOR CHILDREN OF DIVORCE   R3-8

1. You have the right to ask to see each of your parents.

2. You have the right to talk to each of your parents on the phone as often as you like.

3. You have the right to refuse to deliver unkind messages from one parent to another.

4. You have the right to request private time with your parents without their boyfriends or girlfriends (husbands or wives).

5. You have the right to spend time with a visiting parent even if it isn't in the divorce decree.

6. You have the right to see all of your grandparents even if your parents don't like them.

7. You have the right to ask people (a parent, grandparent, or stepparent) to stop talking badly about the absent parent.

8. You have the right to leave any situation in which people refuse to stop talking badly about the absent parent.

9. You have the right to buy cards or gifts for any of your relatives (aunts, uncles, grandparents, stepparents, siblings, stepsiblings).

10. You have the right to request to live with a different parent.

11. You have the right to keep things to yourself (privacy).

12. You have the right to say "Don't ask me who I love more."

13. You have the right to refuse to spy on one parent for the other parent.

14. You have the right to talk about things that may bother you with such appropriate individuals as school guidance personnel or your minister.

15. Know what constitutes physical and sexual abuse—you have the right to avoid abuse.

16. You have the right to discuss your reasons for not wanting to see a parent.

17. You have the right to request a change in the visitation schedule if it interferes with such things as school activities or a part-time job.

18. You have the right to like your stepparents and stepsiblings.

# WHAT YOU CAN DO WHEN YOUR RIGHTS HAVE BEEN VIOLATED
## Good Communication Skills are a Major Factor in Maintaining Rights   R3-9

1.  State your case.

    When you feel that you have been treated unfairly, tell the person how you feel. You need to be direct in your approach and clear about your reasons. Be constructive (tell the person how you want to be treated). Use this approach only when necessary. If you do it often, you may be seen as a complainer and you'll be ignored!

    Example: Your mother never writes anything down when your friends call. Your messages consist of "Someone called while you were out." You, on the other hand, always get the name and number of people who call and leave messages for her. What can you say?

2.  Ask for additional information.

    Many times we feel slighted or taken advantage of because we can't see the "big picture." That is, unknown factors may be at work. Asking for additional information clarifies misunderstandings and may give you additional information upon which to base your own assessment of a situation. Having all relevant information can make an unpleasant situation more tolerable.

    Caution: The *way* you ask for additional information is important. "Why" questions can make people defensive and lead to arguments and anger. Use a nonthreatening approach.

    Example: Your father fails to show up for a play in which you have the lead role. He has also failed to show up on regular visiting days for the past several months. Ask him about these things.

3.  Ask a person to stop doing something that hurts your feelings or is annoying.

    Many people are unaware of the effect they are having on the people around them (like the person who absentmindedly clicks his pen during a test). They may not realize that what they said or did hurt your feelings or made you angry. Asking someone to change their behavior can, however, be threatening and they may respond in an angry or aggressive manner, so be tactful in your approach.

    Example: Your mother has begun dating someone who she seems very attached to. For the last month, they have been coming home late at night and making love in the bedroom which is right next to yours. You feel very uncomfortable listening to them. Ask her to be more considerate of your needs.

# WHAT YOU CAN DO WHEN YOUR RIGHTS HAVE BEEN VIOLATED

## Good Communication Skills are a Major Factor in Maintaining Rights (continued)

4. Learn to say "No"!

   Many individuals get taken advantage of because they feel guilty if they refuse to do something for someone. It is possible to say "no" in a polite way. Usually, offering an honest explanation (not an excuse) will suffice.

   Example: Your stepsister, whom you're trying desperately to get along with, asks you for the fifth night in a row to do the dishes for her, even though it's her week to do them. How do you tell her 'no'?

Name _____     Date _____

# WORKING THROUGH CONFLICT   R3-11

1. Discussion.

    Discussion means that all parties have an opportunity to state their concerns. The opposing views must be defined clearly, all parties involved need to understand all relevant issues.

2. Evaluation.

    Weigh both sides of the argument to decide how big the differences of opinion are.

    If the differences are small, a little compromise on the part of both parties may resolve the conflict.

3. Bargaining.

    If compromise is possible, decide what each party will do and state clearly what the terms of the agreement are.

4. Follow through.

    Once an agreement has been made, follow through on the terms of the agreement. This will make future conflicts easier to resolve.

5. Closure.

    If an agreement has been reached, keep the lines of communication open. Show your willingness to hold up your end of the bargain and monitor the progress that the other party is making toward fulfilling its part of the bargain. If the differences are very large, no compromise may be possible. Further discussion will result in argument. Closure is established by restating your position and acknowledging that you feel no agreement can be reached.

Name _____ Date _____

# Relaxation Instructions   R3-13

Gaining conscious control over your body can help reduce the discomfort you feel during times of stress due to physical responses such as as heart palpitations, sweating palms, and quivering voices.

I.  Positioning the Body.

When you are ready to do the relaxation exercises, sit in a comfortable chair. Do not lie down as falling asleep is not what is intended. Sit with both feet flat on the floor or with feet crossed at the ankles. Lace your fingers together and place them in your lap. Focus your eyes on a spot on the floor about eight feet in front of you with your head tipped slightly forward. Now close your eyes.

II. Relaxing your muscles.

In order to tell your muscles to relax, you must know the difference between what it feels like when your muscles are tight, and how they feel when relaxed. Begin tightening and relaxing various groups of muscles. Start at the head by tightening and relaxing the facial muscles (frown). Do this several times. Now do the same thing with the muscles of the neck, then the shoulders and arms. Tighten the stomach muscles and buttocks. Last, tighten and relax the muscles of the thigh and calf.

III. Breathing.

Breathe in as you tighten muscles. Breathe out as you relax the muscles. Imagine yourself becoming more and more relaxed every time you exhale.

With practice, you will be able to relax your entire body by inhaling deeply and relaxing as you slowly exhale breath. It will not be necessary to tighten and relax all the muscle groups.

IV. Imagining.

When your body is comfortable and relaxed, try to imagine the most relaxing scene you can think of. Put yourself in the picture, and feel each sensation. Let go of tension.

Relaxation for self-control is not only helpful for divorce-related problems. Relaxation can also be used when you are angry at a friend, are in a stressful situation such as giving a speech, or are faced with other types of job or school-related stressors such as test anxiety. In short, it can and should be used anywhere, at anytime.

# STUDENT EVALUATION FORM   R3-20

Did you enjoy participating in this group? _____ Yes _____ No

Would you like the group to continue to meet? _____ Yes _____ No

What things did you find most useful about the group? _____

_____

_____

_____

What things would you like to change about the group? _____

_____

_____

_____

Did you feel that you had enough opportunities to discuss your personal
situation? _____ YES _____ NO

What would you like to discuss in future sessions if the group were to continue to meet? ____

_____

_____

_____

Do you have any suggestions for the group leader? _____

_____

_____

_____